TOP▷REQUESTED

23 POPULAR AND TRADITIONAL FAVORITES ARRANGED BY DAN COATES

Contents

Produced by
Alfred Music Publishing Co., Inc.
P.O. Box 10003
Van Nuys, CA 91410-0003
alfred.com

Printed in USA.

ISBN-10: 0-7390-9439-4
ISBN-13: 978-0-7390-9439-6
Cover photo: Kilcoe Castle, Ireland © Shutterstock / Patryk Kosmider

Alfred Cares. Contents printed on 100% recycled paper.

THE BLACK VELVET BAND

Traditional Irish Folk Song
Arranged by Dan Coates

Verse 3:
Next morning before judge and jury
For a trial I had to appear,
And the judge, he said, "You young fellows
The case against you is quite clear.
And seven long years is your sentence,
You're going to Van Dieman's Land
Far away from your friends and relations
To follow the black velvet band."
(To Chorus:)

Verse 4:
So come all you jolly young fellows,
I'd have you take warning by me:
Whenever you're out on the liquor, me lads,
Beware of the pretty colleen.
She'll fill you with whiskey and porter
Until you're not able to stand
And the very next thing that you'll know, me lads,
You're landed in Van Dieman's Land.
(To Chorus:)

DANNY BOY

(Londonderry Air)

Traditional
Arranged by Dan Coates

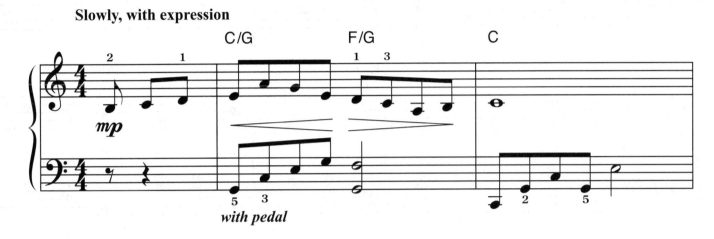

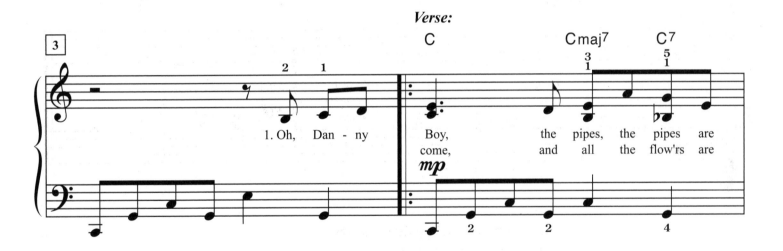

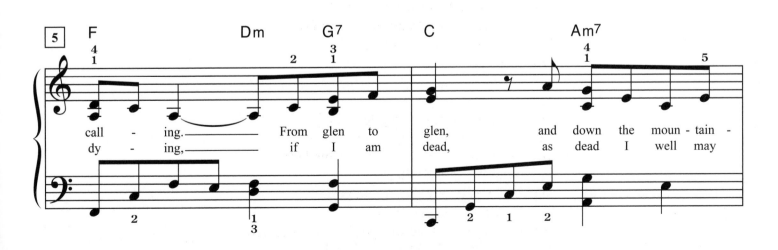

CLANCY LOWERED THE BOOM

Words and Music by
JOHNNY LANGE and HY HEATH
Arranged by Dan Coates

Chorus:

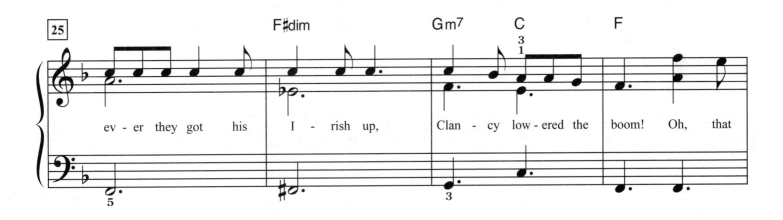

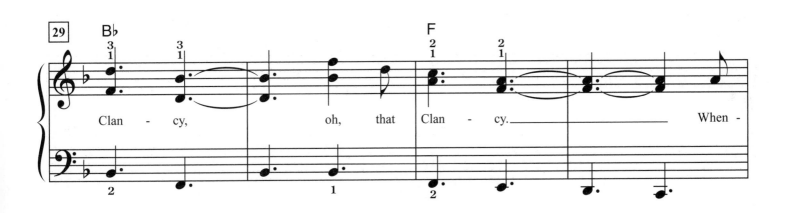

ev - er they got his I - rish up, Clan - cy low - ered the

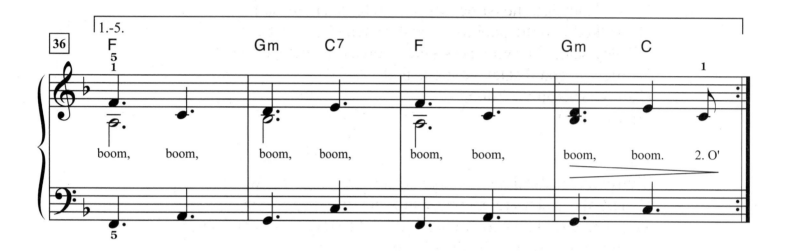

boom, boom, boom, boom, boom, boom, boom, boom. 2. O'

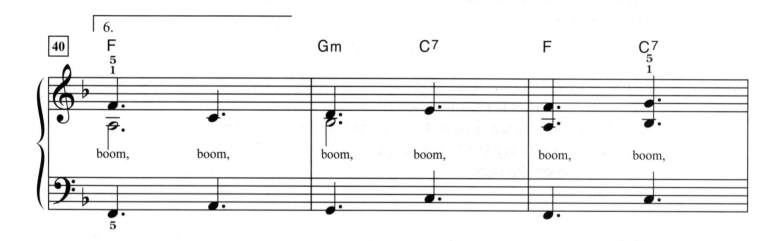

boom, boom, boom, boom, boom, boom,

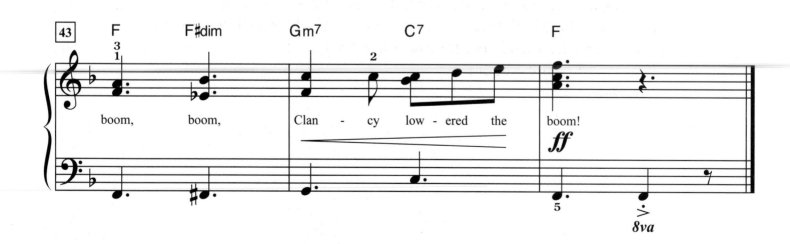

boom, boom, Clan - cy low - ered the boom!

Verse 2:
O'Leary was a fighting man, they all knew he was tough,
He strutted 'round the neighborhood a-shootin' off his guff.
He picked a fight with Clancy, then and there he sealed his doom,
Before you could shout "O'Leary look out!"
Clancy lowered the boom!
(To Chorus:)

Verse 3:
Now Clancy left the barber shop, with tonic on his hair,
He walked into the pool room, and he met O'Riley there.
O'Riley said: "For goodness sakes, now do I smell perfume?"
Before you could stack your cue in the rack,
Clancy lowered the boom!
(To Chorus:)

Verse 4:
Mulrooney walked into the bar, and ordered up a round,
He left his drink to telephone, and Clancy drank it down.
Mulrooney said: "Who drunk me drink? I'll lay him in his tomb!"
Before you could pat the top of your hat,
Clancy lowered the boom!
(To Chorus:)

Verse 5:
O'Hollihan delivered ice to Misses Clancy's flat,
He'd always linger for a while, to talk of this and that.
One day he kissed her, just as Clancy walked into the room,
Before you could say the time of day,
Clancy lowered the boom!
(To Chorus:)

Verse 6:
The neighbors all turned out for Kate O'Grady's wedding night,
McDugal said: "Let's have some fun, I think I'll start a fight!"
He wrecked the hall, then kissed the bride, and pulverized the groom,
Then, quick as a wink, before you could think,
Clancy lowered the boom!
(To Chorus:)

COCKLES AND MUSSELS

(Molly Malone)

Traditional Irish Song
Arranged by Dan Coates

Slowly

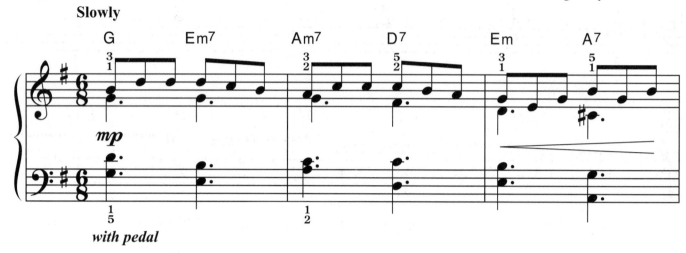

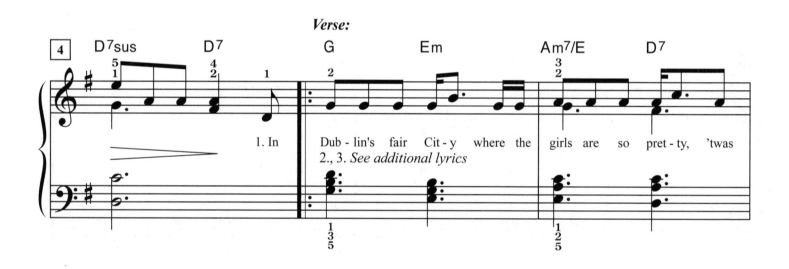

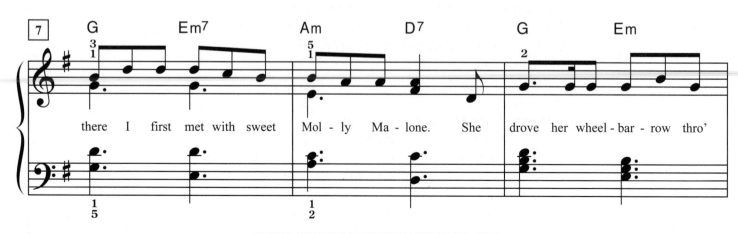

Verse 2:
She was a fish monger, but sure 'twas no wonder,
Her father and mother were fish mongers, too.
They drove wheelbarrows thro' streets broad and narrow,
Crying, "Cockles and mussels, alive, all alive."
(To Chorus:)

Verse 3:
She died of the fever, and nothing could save her,
And that was the end of sweet Molly Malone.
But her ghost drives a barrow thro' streets broad and narrow,
Crying, "Cockles and mussels, alive, all alive."
(To Chorus:)

I'LL TAKE YOU HOME AGAIN, KATHLEEN

Words and Music by
THOMAS P. WESTENDORF
Arranged by Dan Coates

Moderately slow, with expression
Verse:

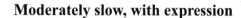

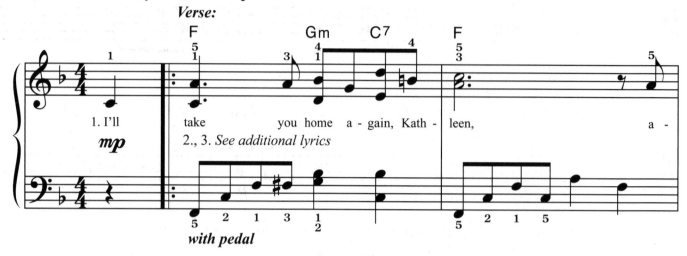

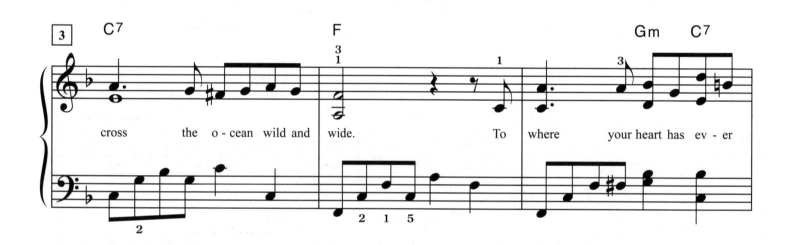

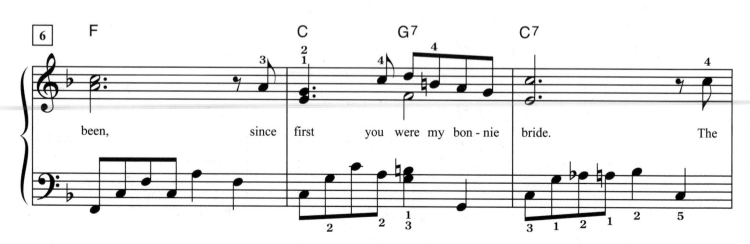

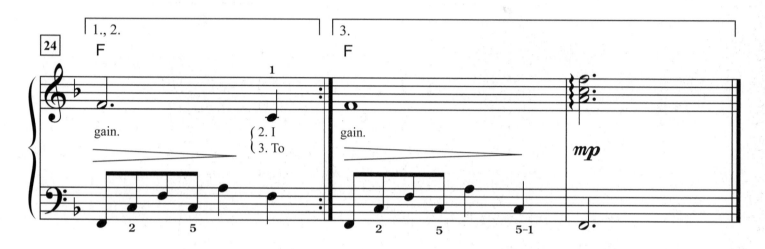

Verse 2:
I know you love me, Kathleen, dear.
Your heart was ever fond and true;
I always feel when you are near,
That life holds nothing dear, but you.
The smiles that once you gave to me,
I scarcely ever see them now.
Tho' many, many times I see
A darkening shadow on your brow.
(To Chorus:)

Verse 3:
To that dear home beyond the sea,
My Kathleen shall again return,
And when thy old friends welcome thee,
Thy loving heart will cease to yearn.
Where laughs the little silver stream,
Beside your mother's humble cot,
And brightest rays of sunshine gleam,
There all your grief will be forgot.
(To Chorus:)

IRISH WEDDING SONG

Words and Music by
IAN BETTERIDGE
Arranged by Dan Coates

God bless this cou - ple who mar - ry to - day.

Chorus:

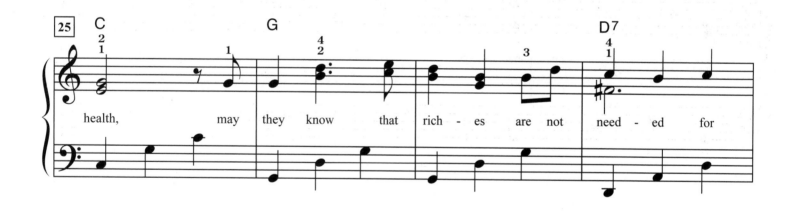

In good times and bad times, in sick - ness and

health, may they know that rich - es are not need - ed for

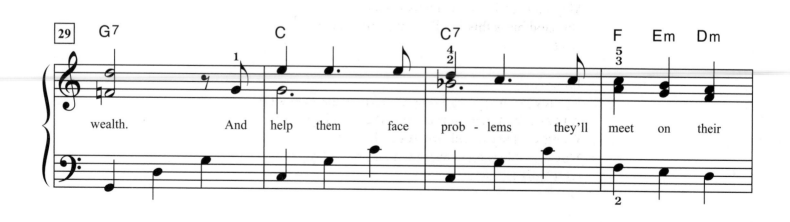

wealth. And help them face prob - lems they'll meet on their

Verse 2:
May they find peace of mind comes to all who are kind.
May the rough times ahead become triumphs in time.
May their children be happy each day.
Oh, God bless this family that started today.
(To Chorus:)

Verse 3:
As they go, may they know every love that was shown.
And as life, it gets shorter, may their feelings grow.
Wherever they travel, wherever they stay,
May God bless this couple who marry today.
(To Chorus:)

THE IRISH ROVER

Traditional Irish Folk Song
Arranged by Dan Coates

Verse 2:
We had one million bags of the Sligo rags,
We had two million barrels of bones.
We had three million sides of old blind horses' hides,
We had four million barrels of stones.
We had five million hogs and six million dogs,
Seven million barrels of porter.
We had eight million bales of old nanny goats' tails
In the hold of the Irish Rover.

Verse 3:
There was Mickey Coote who played hard on his flute
And the ladies lined up for a set.
He would tootle with skill for each sparkling quadrille,
Though the dancers were fluther'd and bet.
With his smart witty talk he was cock of the walk,
As he rolled the dames under and over.
They all knew at a glance when he took up his stance
That he sailed in the Irish Rover.

Verse 4:
There was Barnery McGee from the banks of the Lee
There was Hogan from County Tyrone,
There was Johnny McGurk who was scared stiff to work
And a man from Westmeath called Malone.
There was Slugger O'Toole who was drunk as a rule,
And fighting Bill Tracy from Dover,
And your man, Mick McCann from the banks of the Bann
Was the skipper of the Irish Rover.

Verse 5:
We had sailed seven years when the measles broke out
And the ship lost its way in the fog.
And that whale of a crew was reduced down to two:
Just myself and the Captain's old dog.
Then the ship struck a rock, Oh Lord! what a shock!
The bulkhead was turned right over.
Turned nine times around and the poor dog was drowned.
I'm the last of the Irish Rover.

IRISH WASHERWOMAN

Traditional Irish Jig
Arranged by Dan Coates

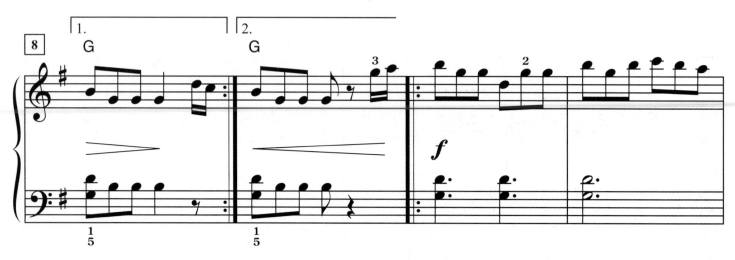

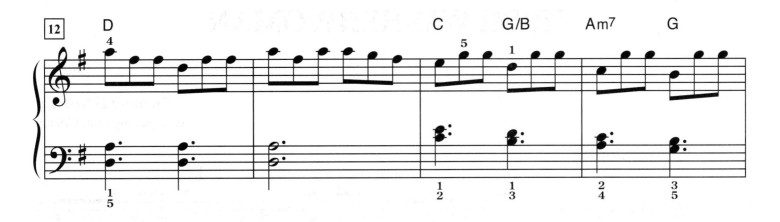

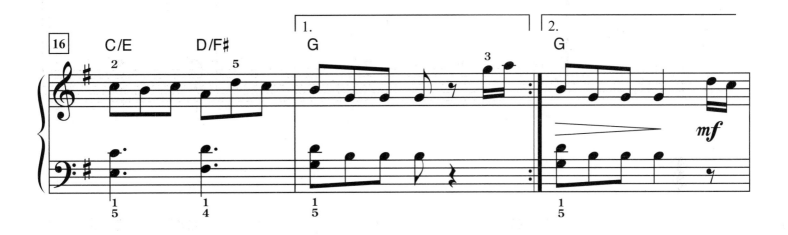

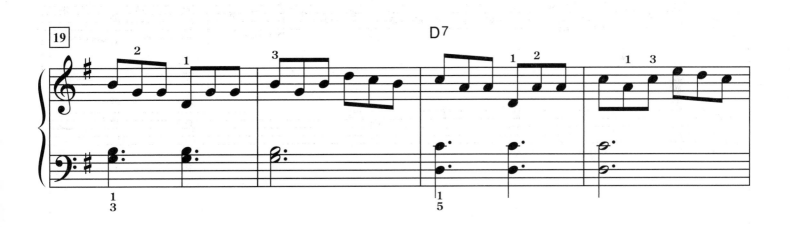

OLD IRISH BLESSING

Words and Music by
DENES AGAY
Arranged by Dan Coates

Calmly, with expression
Chorus:

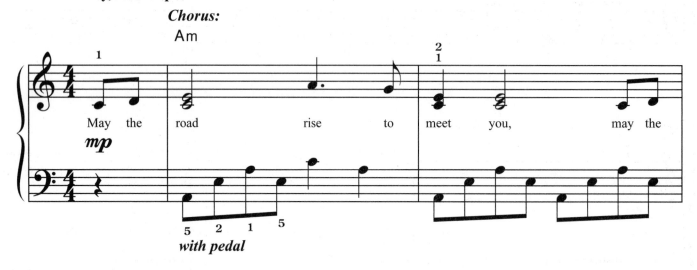

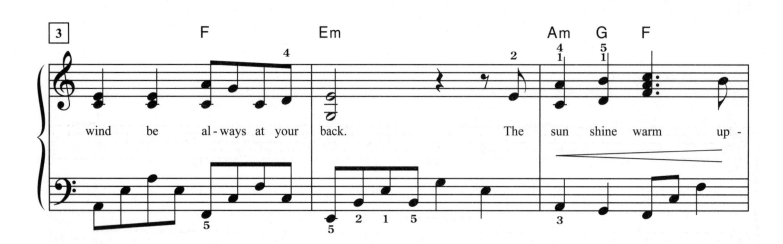

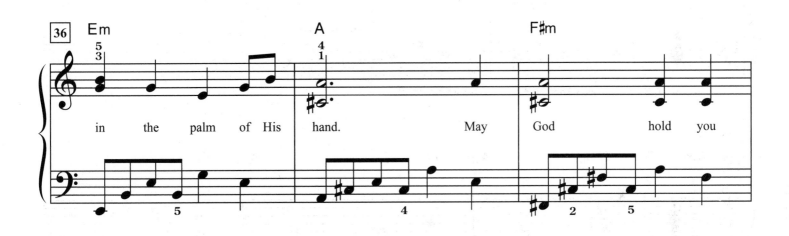

IT'S A GREAT DAY FOR THE IRISH

Words and Music by
ROGER EDENS
Arranged by Dan Coates

Bright march tempo

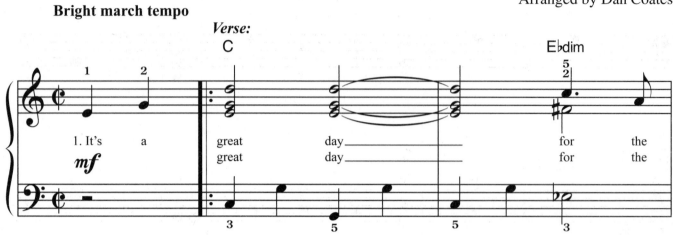

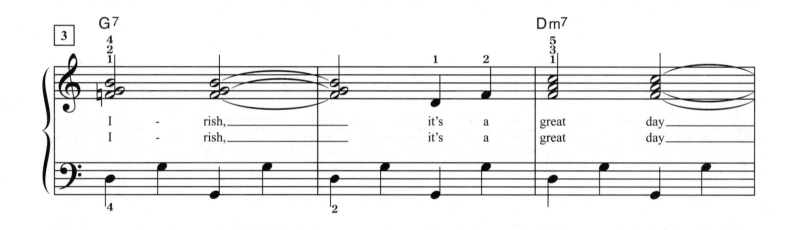

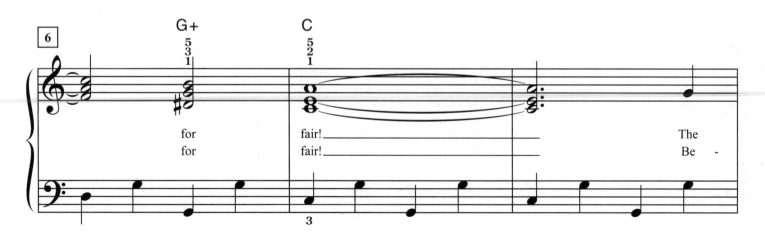

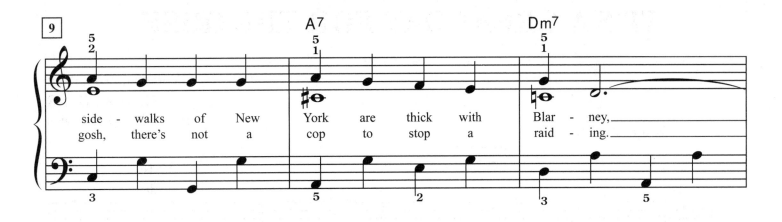

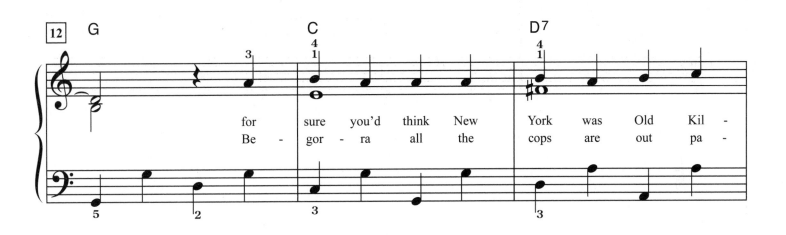

THE KERRY DANCE

Traditional Irish Song
Arranged by Dan Coates

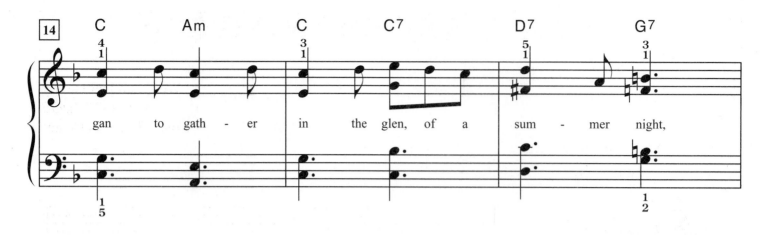

gan   to   gath - er   in   the   glen,   of   a   sum - mer   night,

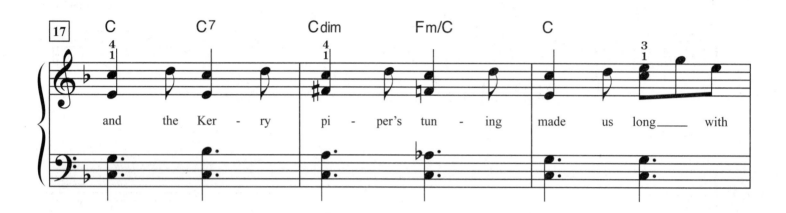

and   the   Ker - ry   pi - per's   tun - ing   made   us   long____   with

Chorus:

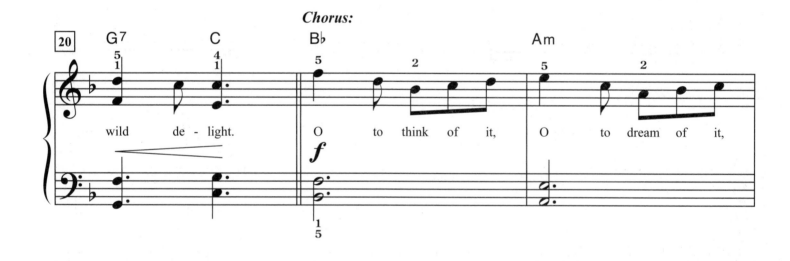

wild   de - light.   O   to   think   of   it,   O   to   dream   of   it,

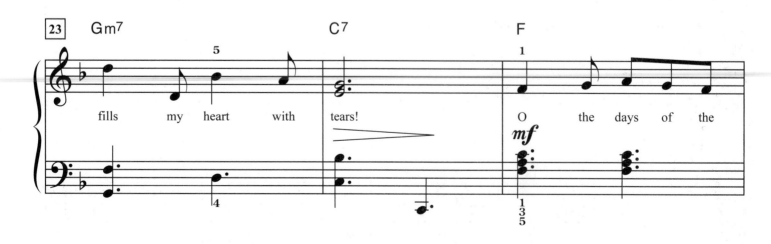

fills   my   heart   with   tears!   O   the   days   of   the

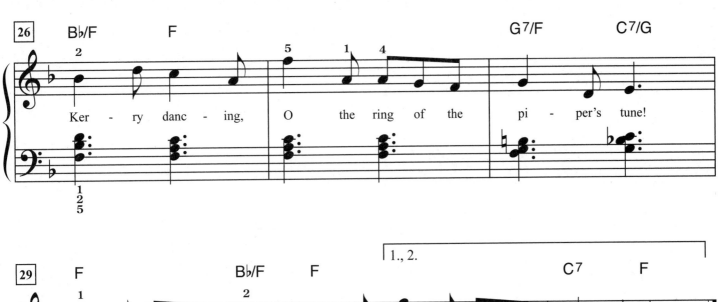

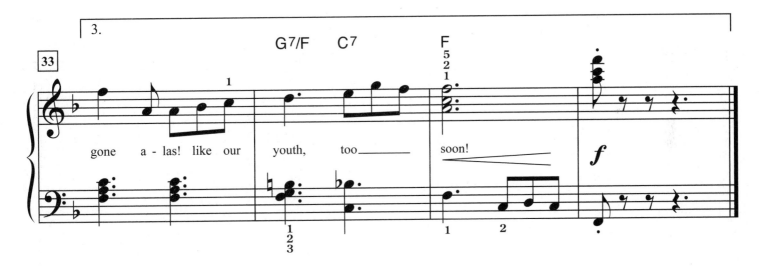

Verse 2:
Was there ever a sweeter colleen in the dance than Eily Moore!
Or a prouder lad than Thady, as he boldly took the floor.
"Lads and lasses to your places, up the middle and down again."
Ah! the merry hearted laughter ringing thro' the happy glen.
(To Chorus:)

Verse 3:
Loving voices of old companions, stealing out of the past once more,
And the sound of the dear old music, soft and sweet as in days of yore.
When the boys began to gather in the glen of a summer night,
And the Kerry piper's tuning made us long with wild delight.
(To Chorus:)

MOTHER MACHREE

Words and Music by
CHANCELLOR OLCOTT
Arranged by Dan Coates

Moderately, with expression
Verse:

MY WILD IRISH ROSE

Words and Music by
CHANCELLOR OLCOTT
Arranged by Dan Coates

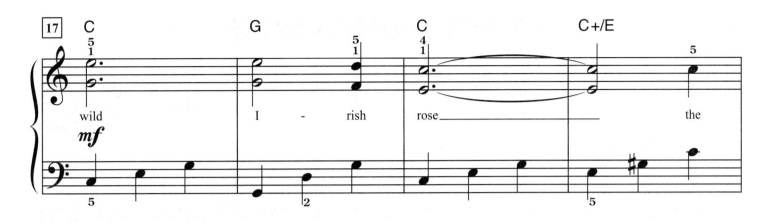

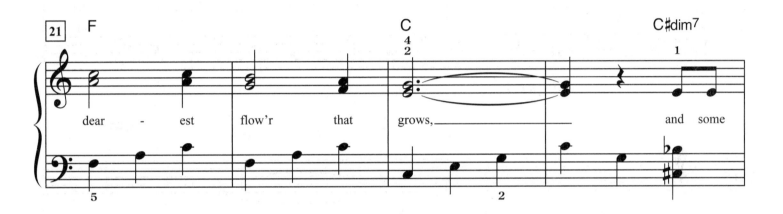

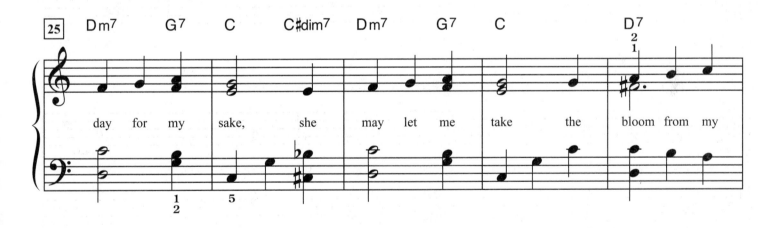

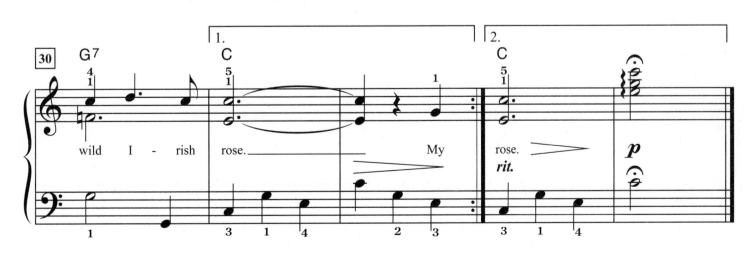

THE PARTING GLASS

Traditional Irish Folk Song
Arranged by Dan Coates

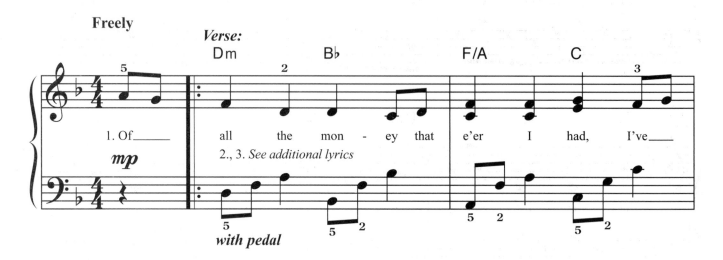

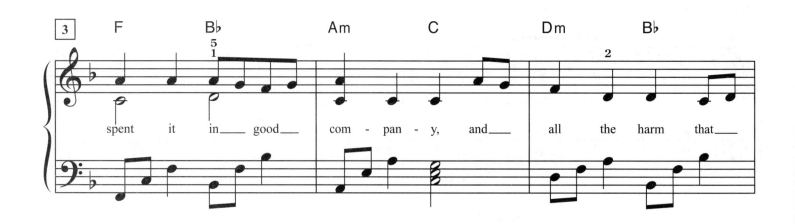

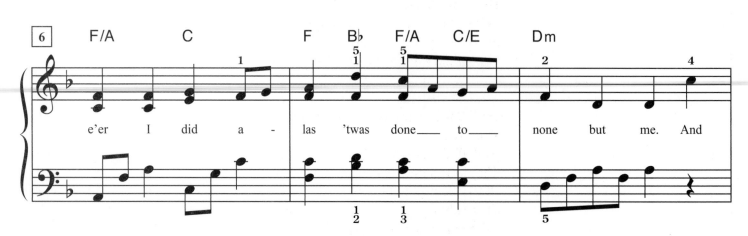

Verse 2:

If I had money enough to spend,
And leisure time to sit awhile,
There is a fair maid in the town
Who sorely has my heart beguiled.
Her rosy cheeks and ruby lips
I own she has my heart in thrall.
So fill to me the parting glass,
Goodnight and joy be with you all.

Verse 3:

Oh, all the comrades that e'er I had,
They're sorry for my going away,
And all the sweet hearts that e'er I had,
They'd wish me one more day to stay.
But since it fall unto my lot
That I should go and you should not,
I'll gently rise and softly call
Goodnight and joy be with you all.

SEVEN DRUNKEN NIGHTS

Traditional Irish Folk Song
Arranged by Dan Coates

Verse 2:
Now, as I came home on Tuesday night,
As drunk as drunk could be,
I saw'r a coat behind the door
Where my old coat should be.
So I called the wife and I said to her,
"Will ya kindly tell to me,
Who owns that coat behind the door
Where my old coat should be?"

Chorus 2:
Ah, you're drunk, you're drunk you silly old fool,
Till you cannot see.
That's a lovely blanket that me mother sent to me.
Well, many's the day I traveled a hundred miles or more,
But buttons on a blanket sure I never seen before.

Verse 3:
And as I went home on Wednesday night,
As drunk as drunk could be,
I saw'r a pipe upon the chair
Where my old pipe should be.
I calls the wife and I says to her
"Will ya kindly tell to me,
Who owns that pipe upon the chair
Where my old pipe should be?"

Chorus 3:
Ah, you're drunk, you're drunk you silly old fool,
Still you cannot see.
And that's a lovely tin whistle that me mother sent to me.
Well, and many's the day I've traveled a hundred miles or more,
But tobacco in a tin whistle sure I never seen before.

Verse 4:
And as I went home on Thursday night,
As drunk as drunk could be,
I saw'r two boots beneath the bed
Where my two boots should be.
I called the wife and I said to her,
"Will ya kindly tell to me,
Who owns those boots beneath the bed
Where my old boots should be?"

Chorus 4:
Ah, you're drunk, you're drunk, you silly old fool,
Until you cannot see.
And that's me lovely geranium pots me mother sent to me.
Well, it's many the day I've traveled a hundred miles or more,
But laces on a geranium pot I never seen before.

Verse 5:
And as I went home on Friday night,
As drunk as drunk could be,
I saw'r a head upon the bed
Where my old head should be.
So, I called the wife and I said to her,
"Will you kindly tell to me,
Who owns that head upon the bed
Where my old head should be?"

Chorus 5:
Ah, you're drunk, you're drunk you silly old fool,
And still you cannot see.
That's a baby boy that me mother sent to me.
Hey, it's many's the day I've traveled a hundred miles or more,
But a baby boy with whiskers on I never seen before.

THE ROCKY ROAD TO DUBLIN

Traditional Irish Folk Song
Arranged by Dan Coates

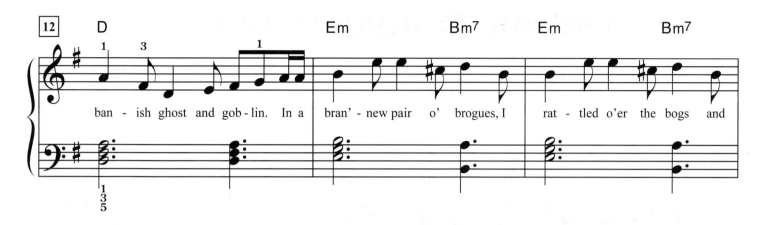

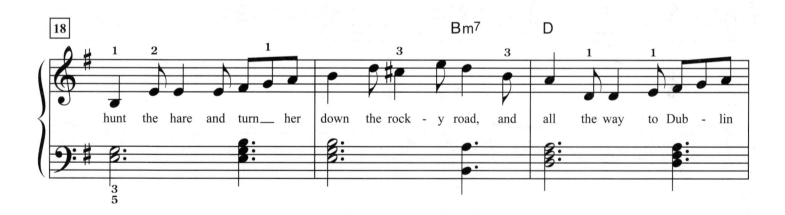

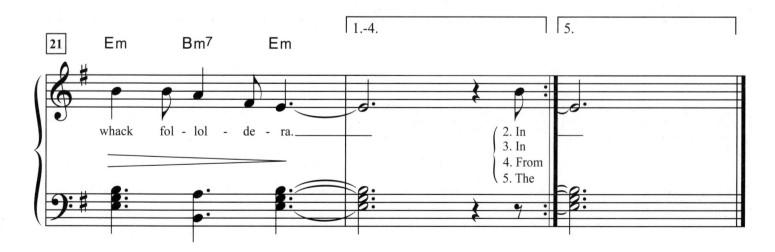

Verse 2:
In Mullingar that night I rested limbs so weary
Started by daylight next morning bright and early
Took a drop of the pure to keep me heart from sinking;
That's a Paddy's cure whenever he's on drinking
See the lassies smile, laughing all the while
At me darlin' style, 'twould set your heart a bubblin'
Asked me was I hired, wages I required
Till I was almost tired of the rocky road to Dublin.
(To Chorus:)

Verse 3:
In Dublin next arrived, I thought it be a pity
To be soon deprived a view of that fine city.
Decided to take a stroll, all among the quality;
Me bundle it was stole, all in a neat locality.
Something crossed me mind, when I looked behind,
No bundle could I find upon me stick a wobblin'
Enquiring for the rogue, they said me Connaught brogue
Wasn't much in vogue on the rocky road to Dublin.
(To Chorus:)

Verse 4:
From there I got away, me spirits never falling,
Landed on the quay, just as the ship was sailing.
The Captain at me roared, said that no room had he;
When I jumped aboard, a cabin found for Paddy.
Down among the pigs, played some funny rigs,
Danced some hearty jigs, the water round me bubbling;
When off to Holyhead wished meself was dead,
Or better far instead on the rocky road to Dublin.
(To Chorus:)

Verse 5:
The boys of Liverpool, when we were safely landed,
Called meself a fool, I could no longer stand it.
Blood began to boil, temper I was losing;
Poor old Erin's Isle they began abusing.
"Hurrah me soul!" says I, let the shillelagh fly.
Some Galway boys were nigh and saw I was a hobblin',
With a loud "hurray!" joined in the fray.
Soon we cleared the way on the rocky road to Dublin.
(To Chorus:)

THE LAST ROSE OF SUMMER

Traditional Irish Melody
Lyrics by THOMAS MOORE
Arranged by Dan Coates

TOO-RA-LOO-RA-LOO-RAL

(That's an Irish Lullaby)

Words and Music by
J.R. SHANNON
Arranged by Dan Coates

THE WEARING OF THE GREEN

Traditional Irish Ballad
Arranged by Dan Coates

Moderately bright

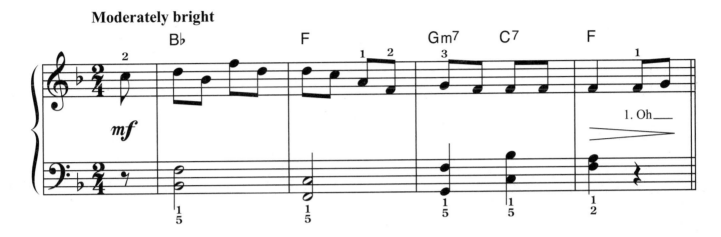

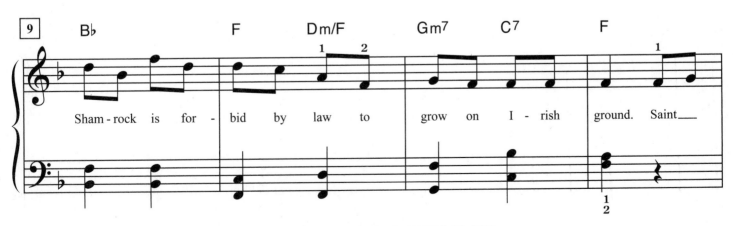

13 Pat - rick's Day no more we'll keep, his col - or can't be seen, for

Gm7 C7

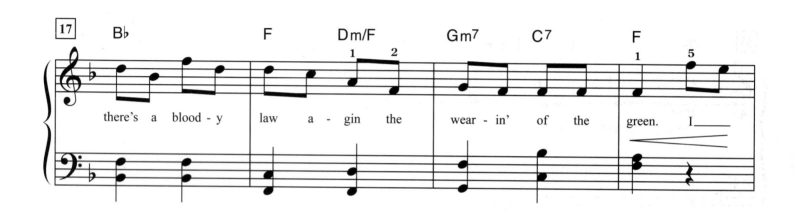

17 B♭ F Dm/F Gm7 C7 F

there's a blood - y law a - gin the wear - in' of the green. I____

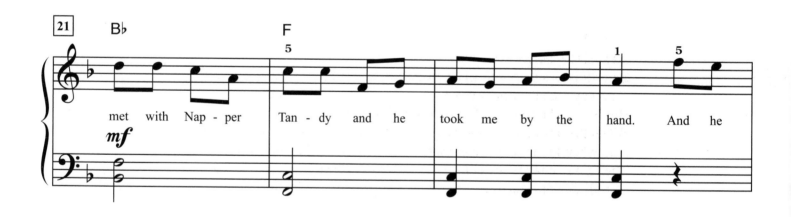

21 B♭ F

met with Nap - per Tan - dy and he took me by the hand. And he

mf

25 B♭ F G7 C

said, "How's poor old Ire - land, and how____ does she stand? She's the

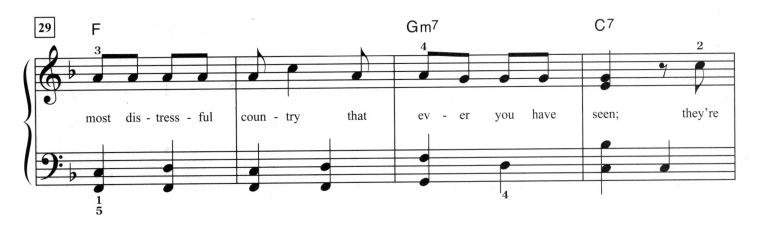

most dis - tress - ful | coun - try | that | ev - er you have | seen; | they're

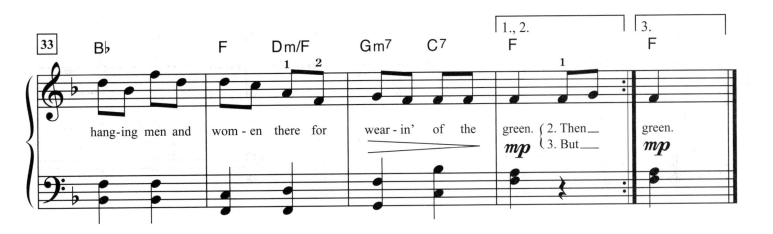

hang-ing men and | wom - en there for | wear - in' of the | green. { 2. Then___ / 3. But___ | green.

Verse 2:

Then since the color we must wear is England's cruel red,
Sure Ireland's sons will ne'er forget the blood that they have shed;
You may take the Shamrock from your hat and cast it on the sod,
But 'twill take root and flourish still, tho' under foot 'tis trod.
When the law can stop the blades of grass from growing as they grow,
And when the leaves in summertime their verdure dare not show,
Then I will change the color I wear in my caubeen;
But till that day, please God, I'll stick to wearin' of the green.

Verse 3:

But if at last our color should be torn from Ireland's heart,
Her sons with shame and sorrow from the dear old soil will part.
I've heard whisper of a country that lives far beyant the sea,
Where rich and poor stand equal in the light of freedom's day.
Oh! Erin must we leave you driven by the tyrant's hand?
Must we ask a mother's welcome from a strange but happier land
Where the cruel cross of England's thralldom never shall be seen?
And where, thank God, we'll live and die, still wearin' of the green.

WHEN IRISH EYES ARE SMILING

Words by CHAUNCEY OLCOTT
and GEORGE GRAFF, JR.
Music by ERNEST R. BALL
Arranged by Dan Coates

WHISKEY IN THE JAR

Traditional Irish Folk Song
Arranged by Dan Coates

Chorus:

rig um du rum da, whack for my dad - dy - o,___

whack for my dad - dy - o,___ there's whis - key in the jar. 2. I jar.

Verse 2:

I counted out his money and made a pretty penny.
I put it in my pocket and I took it home to Jenny.
She told me that she loved me, and never would deceive me,
But the devil take the women, for they never can be easy.
(To Chorus:)

Verse 3:

I went into my chamber, all for to take a slumber,
I dreamt of gold and jewels and for sure it was no wonder.
That Jenny took my charges and she filled them up with water,
Then sent for Captain Farrel to be ready for the slaughter.
(To Chorus:)

Verse 4:

Twas early in the morning, as I rose up for travel,
The guards were all around me and likewise Captain Farrel.
I first produced my pistol, for she had stole my rapier,
But I couldn't shoot the water so a prisoner I was taken.
(To Chorus:)

Verse 5:

If anyone can aid me, it's my brother in the army,
If I can find his station down in Cork or in Killarney.
And if he'll come and save me, we'll go roving near Kilkenny,
I swear he'll treat me better than my darling sportling Jenny.
(To Chorus:)

Verse 6:

Now some men take delight, in drinking and in roving,
But others take delight in the gambling and the smoking.
Now I take delight in the juice of the barley,
And courting pretty fair maids in the morning bright and early.
(To Chorus:)

THE WILD ROVER

Traditional Irish Folk Song
Arranged by Dan Coates

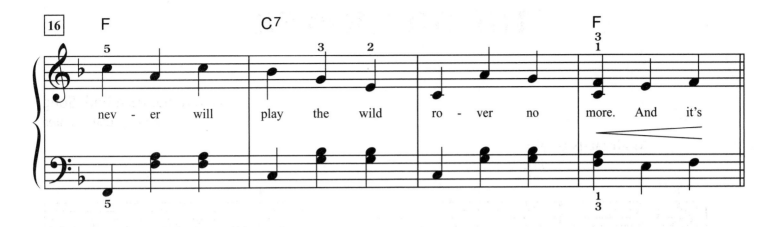

Chorus:

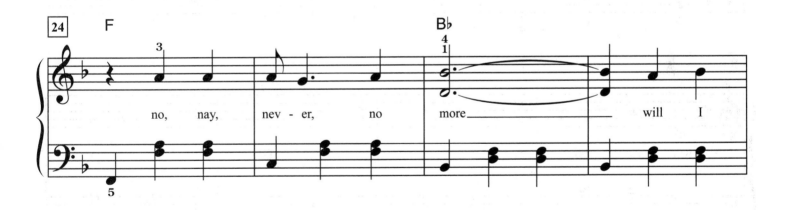

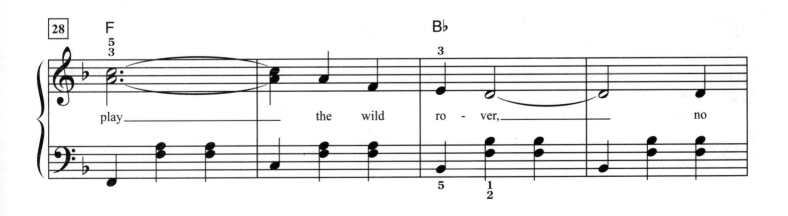

Verse 2:

I went in an alehouse I used to frequent,
And I told the landlady me money was spent.
I asked her for credit, she answered me, "Nay,
Such custom as you I can have any day."
(To Chorus:)

Verse 3:

I took from me pocket ten sovereigns bright
And the landlady's eyes opened wide with delight.
She says, "I have whiskeys and wines of the best,
And the words that I spoke sure were only in jest."
(To Chorus:)

Verse 4:

I'll go home to me parents, confess what I've done,
And I'll ask them to pardon their prodigal son.
And if they caress me, as oft times before,
I never will play the wild rover no more.
(To Chorus:)

YOU RAISE ME UP

Words and Music by ROLF LOVLAND
and BRENDAN GRAHAM
Arranged by Dan Coates

Freely, with expression

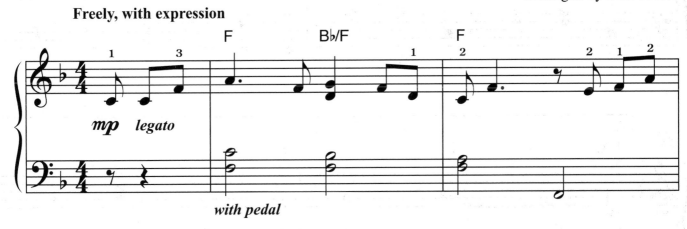

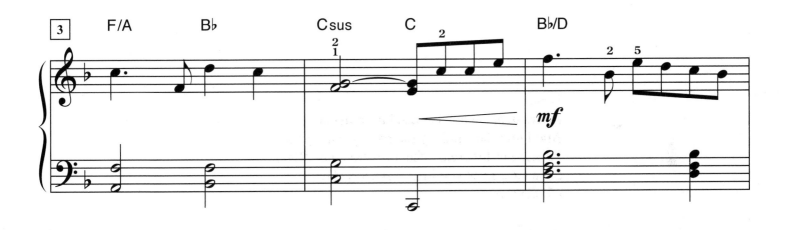

60

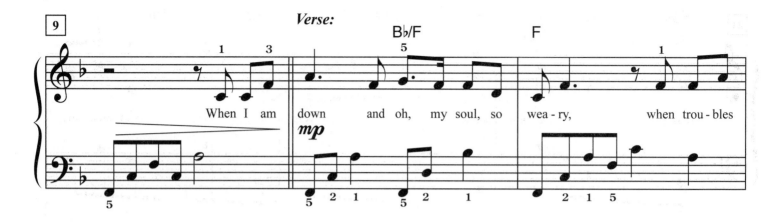

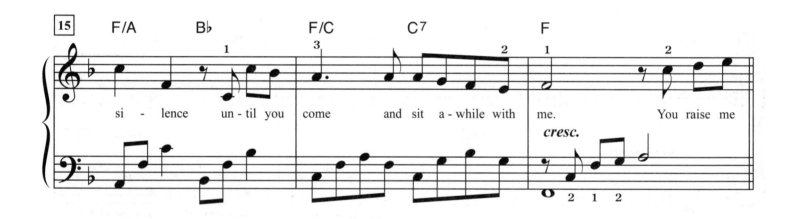

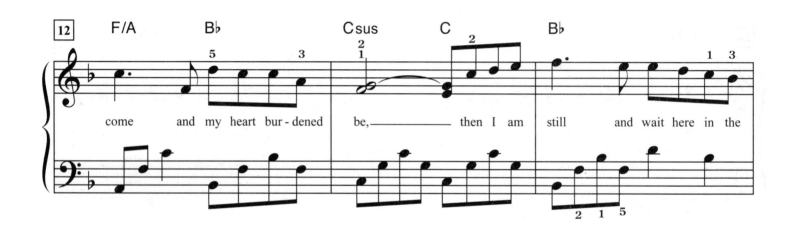

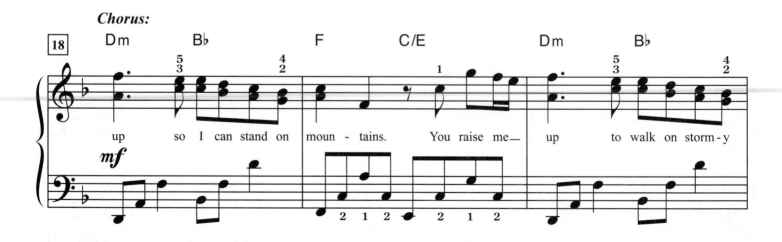

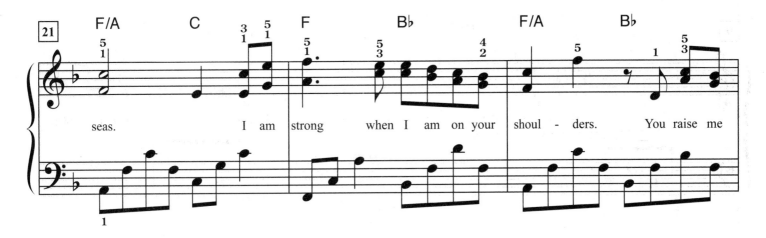

seas.   I am strong   when I am on your shoul - ders.   You raise me

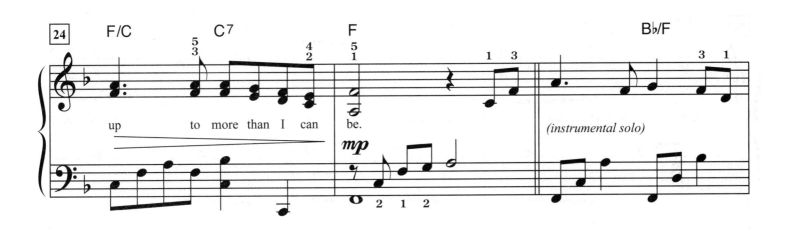

up   to more than I can be.   *(instrumental solo)*

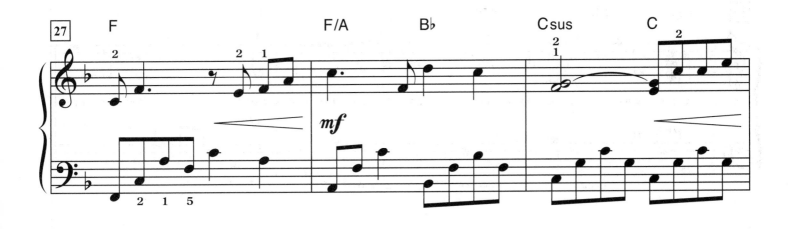

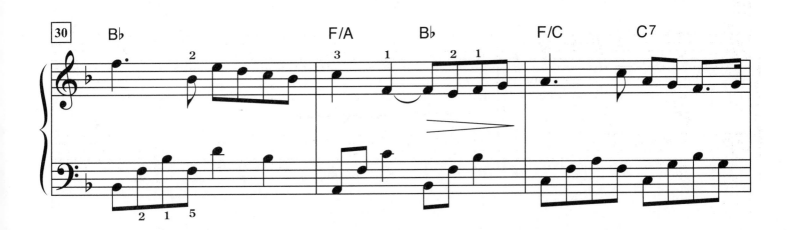

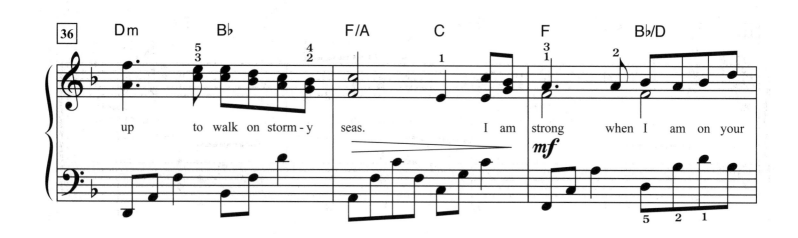

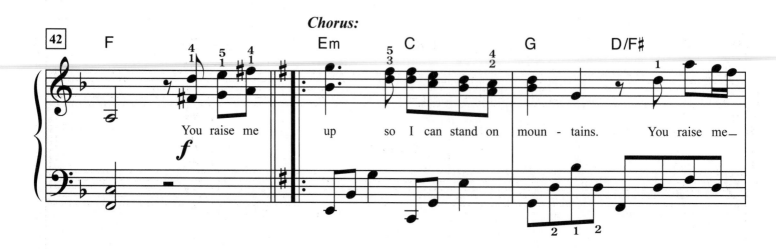

Complete
ICT
for Cambridge IGCSE®
Revision Guide

Stephen Doyle

OXFORD
UNIVERSITY PRESS

OXFORD
UNIVERSITY PRESS

Great Clarendon Street, Oxford, OX2 6DP, United Kingdom

Oxford University Press is a department of the University of Oxford.
It furthers the University's objective of excellence in research, scholarship, and education by publishing worldwide. Oxford is a registered trade mark of Oxford University Press in the UK and in certain other countries

British Library Cataloguing in Publication Data
Data available

978-0-19-835783-4

3 5 7 9 10 8 6 4 2

Paper used in the production of this book is a natural, recyclable product made from wood grown in sustainable forests.
The manufacturing process conforms to the environmental regulations of the country of origin.

Printed in in Great Britain by Bell and Bain Ltd., Glasgow

Acknowledgements
The publishers would like to thank the following for permissions to use their photographs:

p34: Bacho Foto/Fotolia; p35t: hadkhanong/Fotolia; p35m: tbaeff/Fotolia; p35b: rommma/Fotolia; p36: Petr Malyshev/Fotolia; p124a: skaljac/Fotolia; p124b: Onidji/Fotolia; p124c: Kuzmick/Fotolia; p124d: Sergiogen/Fotolia.

Artwork by Six Red Marbles and OUP.

Although we have made every effort to trace and contact all copyright holders before publication this has not been possible in all cases. If notified, the publisher will rectify any errors or omissions at the earliest opportunity.

Links to third party websites are provided by Oxford in good faith and for information only. Oxford disclaims any responsibility for the materials contained in any third party website referenced in this work.

The questions, example answers, marks awarded, and comments that appear in this title were written by the author. In examination, the way marks are awarded to answers like these may be different.

® IGCSE is the registered trademark of Cambridge International Examinations.

Contents

Introduction

This revision guide covers the theory content of Cambridge International Examinations IGCSE® ICT (0417). It also gives you useful advice on the practical part of the syllabus. This book will support you in your revision and will help you achieve your best by offering practical help and guidance on how to approach examination questions.

The main part of the book covers the theoretical part of the course. Towards the end, you will find help and guidance on the practical section. Here are some of the key features you will encounter throughout this revision guide:

SYLLABUS

This gives the syllabus headings covered in the topic.

REVISION SUMMARY

This describes the main concepts and terminology covered in the topic.

Exam preparation

These short exercises will increase your confidence in approaching exam-style questions. Suggested answers can be found at the back of the book.

Exam-style questions

These are exam-style questions for you to try, based on the content in each topic. Sample answers are provided at the back of the book.

Important things to remember

This is a summary of the topic content but with some words missing. Test yourself to see if you can fill in the missing words and phrases. Answers are provided at the back of the book.

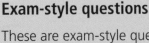  **MINUTE TEST**

This is a short test covering the key concepts and terms covered in the topic. Suggested answers to these are provided at the back of the book.

Exam guidance and practice

These sections will help you prepare for assessment. They contain useful tips and techniques and there are lots of sample exam questions for you to practise. Sample answers are provided at the back of the book.

Revision checklist; practical papers

The detailed content for the practical papers has not been included in this revision guide as the skills needed should be developed over time during your lessons.

However, in this section you will find checklists which allow you to assess your practical skills. By assessing your skills and knowledge you can decide where to focus your efforts. Are there areas where you need further practice?

Glossary

At the end of the revision guide, you will find a glossary containing definitions of key ICT terms.

Best of luck in your examinations and beyond!

Exam guidance and practice 1

What you will learn

There are three assessment objectives for the IGCSE in ICT. You will be assessed on your:

- ability to recall, select and communicate knowledge and understanding of ICT,
- ability to apply knowledge, understanding and skills to produce ICT solutions,
- ability to analyse, evaluate and make reasoned judgements and present conclusions.

You will be required to take three examination papers with each paper covering the following:

Paper 1   Theory

Paper 2   Document Production, Data Manipulation and Presentations

Paper 3   Data Analysis and Website Authoring.

The examination will assess your skills and knowledge of ICT

All questions in each of the papers are compulsory and your answers to all the papers are externally assessed.

Paper	Duration	Coverage	Weighting
1 Theory	2 hours	Assesses theoretical knowledge in Sections 1–21 (i.e. all the sections).	40%
2 Document Production, Data Manipulation and Presentations	2½ hours	Assesses practical skills in Sections 17, 18 and 19.	30%
3 Data Analysis and Website Authoring	2½ hours	Assesses practical skills in Sections 20 and 21.	30%

Answering questions

There are two main things which might limit how well you do in an examination:

- Lack of knowledge
- Lack of examination technique.

It is possible to know a topic very well and yet not do as well as you could because of lack of examination technique. Examination technique is particularly important in ICT because the questions need quite a lot of analysing before answering.

Most importantly, you need to answer:

- the question you have been asked
- not a question you think has been asked
- or the question you would like to have been asked (because you know the answer to it!).

Common mistakes when answering ICT questions

Here is a list of the common mistakes made when answering ICT questions:

- Copying out the question or part of the question in the answer – this just wastes time.
- Writing one word for an answer that requires a sentence.
- Writing a sentence for an answer that requires a one-word answer.
- Writing 'faster, cheaper, better, easier, etc.', in your answers, rather than explaining why.
- The use of brand names on their own such as Word or Access when you should write word-processing software or database software.

Tips for answering questions

In many cases the introductory sentences/paragraphs will refer to a particular business or type of organisation such as a car dealership, a school library, a shop, a doctors' surgery, etc., and the answers you give should relate to the context. Do not write general answers that would apply to any organisation.

Be clear and concise in your answers.

Do not waffle or ramble on. This wastes time. Concentrate on giving facts, not flowery prose.

The average person knows quite a bit about ICT. For IGCSE ICT your knowledge is deeper than this, so your answers to questions need to reflect this.

Questions often contain emboldened details on the number of responses needed. For example, 'Describe **three** ways in which an organisation's own staff can present a security risk for ICT systems'. Make sure that your three answers are distinctly different.

Make sure that you also use some of the knowledge gained from practical work in your answers.

What is a structured question?

A structured question consists of a series of related questions often based on a short paragraph describing a situation. Some questions may require short, one-word answers or a single sentence. Others will require more detailed explanations.

Here is an example of a structured question:

Stergos runs a medium-sized company. His computer network uses a file server which has all the data files and programs stored on it. Stergos is investigating the best method of backing up the data and programs on this server.

A	Describe what is meant by a backup.	*(2 marks)*
B	Give **two** ways in which the original data on the file server could be lost, damaged or destroyed.	*(2 marks)*
C	Stergos has decided to choose between magnetic hard disk and magnetic tape for the taking of backup copies. Discuss the advantages and disadvantages of using each of these media.	*(6 marks)*

The marks for each question will vary according to how much explanation is required in the answers. For example, short answers requiring a very brief statement or definition could earn you 1 or 2 marks. Questions that require longer answers that demonstrate a deeper understanding will usually be awarded more marks.

Identifying what each question requires

In the example structured question on page 2, notice how different words are used at the start of each question to tell you what to do, such as 'describe', 'give' and 'discuss'.

The following words are commands or instructions common to all structured questions. Each one requires you to answer a question in a different way. Some examples of questions are provided.

Commands	What is required?
Compare and contrast	Point out the similarities and differences between two things.
Define	Give a definition of a term.
Describe	Provide a series of short descriptions or explain a series of steps. 'A store uses an EFTPOS terminal for stock control. Describe the computer processing that takes place in order to determine if a product needs re-ordering.' 'Describe what is meant by spyware.' 'Describe the differences between physical security and e-safety when using computers.'
Discuss	Describe reasons or arguments for and against a particular proposal. Sometimes you have to weigh up the advantages and disadvantages of two devices, ways of doing things or situations. Usually these are questions requiring longer answers. 'Homes contain many microprocessor-controlled devices. Discuss the effects of these on people's lifestyles.'
Explain	Clearly define and describe what a term/process means. Usually a more extended answer is needed involving several sentences. 'Explain the differences between phishing and pharming.'
Give	Usually a single word or a short sentence. 'CDs or pen drives can be used for transferring work between computers. Give **three** reasons why a student may prefer to use a pen drive.' 'Give **two** uses of expert systems.'
Identify	Find or state the choice. 'Identify **two** input devices which would be used at an EFTPOS terminal.'
Name	Just give the name, which is usually a single word. 'Other than a temperature sensor, name **two** sensors used in a greenhouse.'

How to approach a structured question

Read the introductory sentences/paragraph slowly and then read all the subsequent questions in full before starting your answer.

Make sure you understand as much as you can about each question before you start writing your answer.

Underline all the key terms and concepts you can identify in the extract/ scenario and each question.

Note the command word in each question to identify what is expected from your answer.

We will now apply these techniques to the structured question on page 2.

Stergos runs a <u>medium-sized</u> company. His <u>computer network</u> uses a <u>file server</u> which has all the <u>data files and programs stored</u> on it. Stergos is investigating the best method of <u>backing up</u> the <u>data and programs</u> on this server.

A <u>Describe</u> what is meant by a <u>backup</u>. *(2 marks)*

Do not waste time writing any part of the question out – so, for example, don't start by writing 'The purpose of a backup is…'.

Here is a sample answer with the marks in brackets.

A copy of programs and data files *(1)* kept for security purposes on an alternative medium *(1)* in case the originals are damaged or destroyed *(1)* and kept away from the location of the computer *(1)*.

B <u>Give</u> **two** ways in which the original data on the file server could be <u>lost, damaged or destroyed</u>. *(2 marks)*

'Give' means one-word or several-word answers are ok.

Any two answers from the following would be acceptable:

Fire *(1)*

Theft of hardware *(1)*

Virus attack *(1)*

Equipment malfunction *(1)*

User error *(1)*

C Stergos has decided to choose between <u>magnetic hard disk</u> and <u>magnetic tape</u> for the taking of <u>backup copies</u>.

<u>Discuss</u> the <u>advantages</u> and <u>disadvantages</u> of using each of these media. *(6 marks)*

There are six marks here for advantages and disadvantages, so separate and distinct points are needed. In 'discuss' questions you should provide a conclusion.

Here is an example of a good quality answer, which includes a number of clear advantages and disadvantages, as well as a conclusion:

It is faster to store onto tape when all the files on the server need backing up *(1)*

For the same amount of data, tape storage is cheaper *(1)*

Tapes are easier to store *(1)*

Tapes are easier to remove from the premises as they are separate from the drive *(1)*

Hard disks are mainly situated in the drives which makes them heavy and less portable *(1)*

Tape backup drives are usually included with file servers so no extra device needs to be bought *(1)*

Conclusion: Tape would be best as the capacity is higher, they are more portable and the speed at which data is saved to them is faster as all the files on the server need to be backed up *(1)*

 **20** *MINUTE TEST*

You now have 20 minutes to answer the following structured question using all the techniques you have learned in this section.

1 There are a number of health and safety risks associated with the use of computers.

   A Explain the difference between a health risk and a safety risk. *(2 marks)*

   B Give the names of **three** health risks associated with computer use and describe what a computer user can do to minimise each risk. *(6 marks)*

When you have finished writing your answers, compare them with the sample answers and teacher comments provided on the following pages.

A <u>Explain</u> the <u>difference</u> between a <u>health risk</u> and a <u>safety risk</u>. *(2 marks)*

Sample answer

A health risk is something that makes you unhealthy and a safety risk is something that is dangerous.

Teacher comments

This answers simply repeats a lot of words from the question and is not clear enough to do well.

The student needed to mention that safety usually concerns the things which might cause accidents (e.g. things piled too high that may fall over onto someone, cables lying across the floor as a tripping hazard, etc.) and health risk are things that do not cause accidents but can lead to health problems.

B <u>Give</u> the names of **three** <u>health risks</u> associated with computer use and <u>describe</u> what a computer user can do to minimise each risk. *(6 marks)*

Sample answer

Becoming overweight – do not snack while you are using your computer.

Eye strain – have regular eye tests.

Repetitive strain injury caused by using a keyboard or mouse over a long period without a break – take regular breaks or changes in activity to an activity that does not involve computer use.

Teacher comments

Putting on weight is not really directly caused by computers because this tends to be caused by overeating or lack of exercise.

The second answer is okay but it fails to explain how eye strain is caused by computer use. If the student had mentioned that it was caused by a dirty screen, screen flicker, etc., then I would have given two marks. Only one out of two marks is given.

The third answer is fine as the health risk, how it is caused by computer use and how it can be avoided are mentioned. I'd award two marks here.

So, how good do you think your answers were compared to those of the student and the examiner's comments? For each question, make a note of where you need to improve your answers.

Let's look at another example

Computer viruses are a threat to computer systems.

A Explain what is meant by a computer virus. *(2 marks)*

B Give **one** thing that a computer virus might do on a computer system. *(1 mark)*

C Give **one** way of preventing computer viruses entering a system. *(1 mark)*

Sample answer 1

A A program that does damage.

B Destroy the computer.

C Use McAfee to stop viruses getting into your computer.

Teacher comments

A This is a bit vague because it is not specific about what it does damage to. I would award 1 mark for this answer.

B Not a strong answer. Viruses can be removed and therefore cannot be said to 'destroy' the computer.

C Brand names should never be given. So instead of McAfee they should have said 'antivirus software or virus scanner'.

(1 mark out of 4)

Sample answer 2

A A mischievous program that copies itself onto your computer and does harm by messing up settings or deleting data.

B It can start to make your computer run slowly and can also cause it to crash unexpectedly.

C Use virus scanning software to scan for viruses and remove them if they are found.

Teacher comments

A A good answer which makes it clear that it is a program that copies itself.

B Again another good answer which gives an example of what a virus might do.

C A strong answer.

(4 marks out of 4)

Teacher's suggested answers

A Two marks allocated in the following way:

Program that copies itself automatically (*1*) and causes damage to data or causes the computer to run slowly (*1*).

B One mark for an answer such as:

Can erase files which means the operating system software cannot be loaded (*1*).
Can cause the deletion of data (*1*).
Can cause the computer to crash (*1*).
Can cause the changing of settings, which causes annoyance to the user (*1*).
Can copy passwords and usernames and transmit these to another person (*1*).

C One mark for one of the following:
Don't open file attachments unless you know who they are from. *(1)*
Install virus scanning/checking software. *(1)*
Keep virus scanning/checking software up-to-date. *(1)*
Don't download files from unknown sources. *(1)*

1 Types and components of computer systems

REVISION SUMMARY

→ **Hardware** means the physical components of a computer system (i.e. the parts you can physically touch) whereas **software** are programs for controlling the operation of the computer or the processing of electronic data.

→ Hardware can be either **internal** (inside the computer casing) or **external** (outside the computer casing).

→ **Software** can be divided into **system software** and **applications software**. System software is the collection of programs that control the running of a computer system. Applications software is software that is used to complete a task such as storing student details in a database.

→ The main components of a computer system are the **central processing unit (CPU)**, **internal memory** (ROM and RAM), **input devices**, **output devices** and **secondary/backing storage**.

→ All computers need an **operating system** as part of the system software. Operating systems can use a **command line interface (CLI)** or a **graphical user interface (GUI)**.

→ There is a range of computers to choose from: **desktop computers**, **laptop computers**, **tablet computers** and **smartphones**. Most users connect their computers to **networks**, mainly the internet, using wires/cables or wirelessly using **3G/4G technology**.

→ New technologies are being developed all the time and these are called **emerging technologies** and currently include **artificial intelligence**, **biometrics**, **vision enhancement**, **robotics**, **quantum cryptography**, **computer-assisted translation**, **3D and holographic imaging** and **virtual reality**.

SYLLABUS

This section will

- Detail the types and components of computer systems including hardware and software, the main components, operating systems, types of computer and the impact of emerging technologies.

1.1 Hardware and software

Hardware – can be internal or external

Internal hardware devices are devices inside the computer casing and include the following:

Processor/central processing unit (CPU) – does the processing such as calculations, logic comparisons, sorts, etc.

Motherboard – the main printed circuit board containing the central processing unit and memory and also connectors for connecting external hardware devices such as keyboards, mice, speakers, etc.

Random access memory (RAM) – memory chips which lose their contents when the power is removed.

Read-only memory (ROM) – memory chips where the contents cannot be changed by the user and where the contents are retained when the power is removed.

Video cards – circuits that generate the signals so that a video output device can display computer data such as text and graphics.

Sound cards – an expansion card that allows a computer to send audio signals to audio devices such as speakers or headphones.

Internal hard disk drives – a rigid magnetic material coated disk on which programs and data can be stored.

External hardware devices are those devices outside the computer casing and include monitors, keyboards, mice, printers, scanners, etc., as well as external storage devices such as some optical drives and portable hard disks.

Software

Software consists of sets of instructions that tell the computer hardware what to do.

There are two types of software: system software and applications software.

System software consists of programs that control the computer hardware directly by giving the step-by-step instructions that tell the computer hardware what to do. Here are the components of system software and what they do:

- **Operating system** – controls the system resources and the processes using these resources on a computer. Operating systems control the handling of input, output, interrupts, etc.
- **Device drivers** – short programs used to supply the instructions to the hardware on how to operate devices connected to a computer such as a printer, scanner, etc.
- **Compilers** – software that converts programming language instructions into binary code in one go. The binary code can be understood directly by the computer.
- **Linkers** – link the code (i.e. program instructions) that the programmer writes with other resources and libraries that make up the whole program file.
- **Utilities** – programs to help users with everyday tasks such as: file maintenance, compressing files to make more room, installing and uninstalling software, checking for and removing viruses, etc.

Applications software are programs designed to carry out certain tasks such as keeping accounts, storing and organising student details, producing documents, etc.

1.2 The main components of computer systems

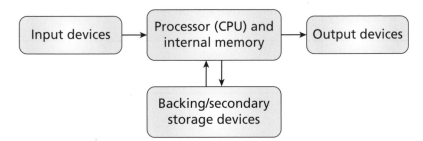

Input devices – include keyboards, mice, microphones, scanners, etc., and are used to enter data into the computer system for processing by the processor.

Processor – sometimes known as the CPU (central processing unit), it is the brain of the computer and it interprets and executes the commands given to it by the hardware and software.

Internal memory – this is where data and instructions are held that are needed immediately by the processor and can be ROM (read only memory) or RAM (random access memory).

Backing/secondary storage devices – this is storage other than internal memory (i.e. RAM and ROM) and includes the internal hard disk, portable hard disk, optical disks, pen drives, etc.

Output devices – such as screens, printers and speakers, and are used to output the results of processing the input data.

ROM (read only memory)	RAM (random access memory)
Data and program instructions are stored permanently.	Data and program instructions are stored temporarily.
The computer can only read the contents.	Can read contents as well as write new contents.
Non-volatile, meaning the contents of memory are retained when there is no power.	Volatile, meaning the contents are lost when there is no power.
Used to store the BIOS program used to boot up the computer when the power is turned on.	

1.3 Operating systems

Operating systems use the following two main ways of interacting with users:

Graphical user interface (GUI) – consisting of **W**indows, **I**cons, **M**enus and **P**ointers (i.e. WIMP for short). Selections are made by clicking a mouse.

Command line interface (CLI) – commands are entered using the keyboard.

Benefits of a GUI	Drawbacks of a GUI
More user friendly.	More hard disk space needed to store operating system.
No commands to remember.	Typing in commands can be faster.
Easy to pass data between software packages.	More RAM and ROM needed.

Benefits of a CLI	Drawbacks of a CLI
Can be faster to type commands than to move and click a mouse.	Commands need to be remembered.
Does not need as much hard disk space as a GUI.	Commands need to be given precisely.
Does not need as much ROM and RAM.	

1.4 Types of computer

There are the following types of computer arranged in order of the largest to the smallest: desktop, laptop, tablet and smartphone.

Most of the exam questions on types of computer are comparative, for example comparing the relative advantages and disadvantages in using a desktop compared to a laptop.

The main features of each are summarised in this table:

Desktop	Laptop	Tablet	Smartphone
Separate components means it is hard to dismantle.	All in one so easy to move.	Light and compact so easily transported.	Very light and pocket sized.
Used on a desk so less likelihood of RSI or backache.	Often used awkwardly so chance of backache or RSI.	Uses an on-screen keyboard which can be awkward to use.	On-screen keyboard is small and hard to use.
Needs a mains power supply.	Can be used away from the mains power.	Can be used away from the mains power.	Can be used away from the mains power.
Easy to upgrade and repair.	Harder to upgrade and repair.	Harder to upgrade and repair.	Harder to upgrade and repair.
Full-sized keyboard and mouse are easy to use.	Touch pad is more cumbersome to use.	Uses a touch screen which makes it easy to surf the net.	Small screen makes it more difficult to use.
Flat surface needed to move mouse on.	No flat surface is needed.	Can be used in most positions including standing up.	Easiest type to use when on the move.

1.5 Impact of emerging technologies

You need to know about the following emerging technologies:

Artificial intelligence (AI) – science of computers learning things to become more intelligent and work things out for themselves.

Biometrics – uses a property of the human body such as fingerprints, pattern on the back of the eye (i.e. the retina) or the pattern on the iris to recognise a person. Can be used for access to phones, buildings, computers and to restrict access at border control at airports and ports.

Computer assisted translation – automatically recognises the language a section of text is in and then converts it into a language you can understand.

Quantum cryptography – uses quantum mechanics to produce a very secure encryption technique. It can detect eavesdroppers and stop the communication.

Vision enhancement – detects light as well as some radiation outside the visible spectrum to produce a clearer image. Used by the military to see in poor light and it can enable people with poor eyesight to see more clearly.

3D and holographic imaging – uses lasers to give the illusion of depth in an image.

Virtual reality – a simulation of the real or an imaginary world. Image is displayed on a headset and you can interact with the system using a keyboard and mouse or using a special glove.

Robotics – robots are used in factories for welding panels, assembling components, paint spraying, moving and packing stock. Robots can be used in the home for vacuuming or washing floors or mowing grass.

Advantages of using robots	Disadvantages of using robots
Can operate continuously 24 hours per day.	Initial purchase cost is high.
You don't have to pay them wages.	Equipment can go wrong.
Can re-program the device to perform different tasks.	Fewer people employed leads to unemployment.
Expensive specialist programmers needed.	
More accurate than humans.	

Exam preparation

1   Use the information contained in the table in Section 1.4 (Types of computer) to compare the benefits and drawbacks of the following different types of computer:

   A   A desktop computer compared to a laptop computer.
   B   A laptop computer compared to a tablet computer.
   C   A tablet computer compared to a smartphone having all the latest features.

Exam-style questions

1   A   Define the terms hardware and software.

   B   Hardware devices can be internal or external. Give the names of **three** internal hardware devices and **three** external hardware devices.

   C   Here are the main components of a computer system:

   Output devices

   Backing/secondary storage devices

   Input devices

   Processor (CPU) and internal memory

   Place each of the above in its correct box in the following diagram of a computer system.

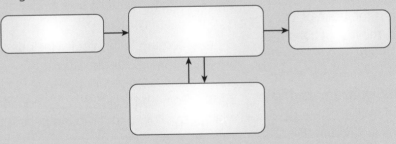

2   Desktop computers and smartphones can be used to access the internet.

   A   Give **two** advantages in using a desktop computer rather than a smartphone for this purpose.

   B   Give **two** disadvantages in using a desktop computer rather than a smartphone for this purpose.

Important things to remember

Fill in the missing key words

Computer systems consist of physical components you can touch called _____ and the instructions, data and programs to tell the computer what to do called _____.

Hardware inside the computer casing (such as the motherboard, RAM and ROM) is called _____ hardware and hardware outside the computer casing (such as keyboards and printers) is called _____ hardware.

Software used to control the computer hardware directly is called _____ software, and that used to accomplish a task such as word proccessing is called _____ software.

_____ driver software gives instructions to the computer as to how to use a new hardware device such as a new printer attached to the computer.

Operating systems, linkers and compilers are examples of _____ software.

The central processing unit is the brain of the computer and it carries out the instructions given to it by the hardware and _____.

There are two types of internal memory: ROM and _____. The BIOS program used to start the computer is stored in _____ which is non-volatile meaning it retains its contents when the power is removed. RAM is _____ meaning it loses its contents when the power is removed, and it is used to hold program instructions and user data currently being worked on.

_____ storage is slower storage and includes the internal hard disk as well as external hard disk, pen drives, tape drives, etc.

Operating systems require an _____ to allow a user to communicate with them and there are two main types: a graphical user interface and a _____ _____ interface. A GUI consists of windows, _____, _____ and pointers and uses a mouse or touch pad to make selections. A command line interface works by the user typing in carefully constructed _____ and this makes it hard to use.

There are a number of _____ methods used to recognise a person to allow them access to buildings, countries or computer resources. One method called _____ scanning uses the unique pattern of blood vessels at the back of the eye and another method called _____ scanning uses the pattern on the coloured area around the pupil to recognise a person. Another method called _____ uses the unique pattern on a finger or thumb to recognise a person.

Other emerging technologies include using quantum physics for quantum _____ which allows very secure transmission of secret information, and _____ enhancement which can allow partially blind people to improve their sight.

_____ are used in factories for the assembly of components, welding, paint-spraying, etc. They have the advantages that they don't need paying, can work _____ without a break and produce high-quality work.

MINUTE TEST

1 Tick true or false next to each of these statements.

	true	false
A graphical user interface is a method of interacting with a user.		
A compiler is an example of system software.		
A laptop computer is usually larger than a desktop computer.		
An icon is part of a command line interface.		
Input devices are examples of hardware.		

2 Tick true or false next to each of these statements.

	true	false
System software is a set of programs and not a single program.		
Command line interfaces are usually considered to be the easiest interface to use.		
One disadvantage in using GUIs is that older computers may need to be upgraded owing to their increased memory and processor requirements.		
Biometric devices are computers that behave like the human brain.		
Graphical user interfaces have features such as windows, icons, menus and pointers.		

3 Describe the differences between the **two** types of internal memory: ROM and RAM.

4 Robots are used in car factories.
   A Describe **two** tasks performed by robots on a car production line.
   B Describe **two** advantages and **two** disadvantages of using robots in car factories.

5 Describe **three** drawbacks of using an operating system that uses a command line interface (CLI).

6 Two emerging technologies are:

   vision enhancement

   biometrics

   Choosing just **one** of the above technologies, explain how it works and how it is used.

2 Input and output devices

REVISION SUMMARY

→ **Input devices** are those devices used to input instructions and data into the computer for processing. All computers come with a **keyboard**, which can be a separate keyboard or an on-screen keyboard found on tablets and smartphones. Most computers use a GUI, which uses a pointing device such as a **mouse** or **touch pad** as an input device to make selections. Sometimes a **trackerball** can be used with a GUI. Other input devices used with desktop and laptop computers, tablets and smartphones include **remote controls, joysticks, touch screens, scanners, digital cameras, microphones, graphics tablets, video cameras** and **web cams**.

→ **Direct data entry (DDE) devices** do not require data to be typed in by someone. Instead they create machine-readable data and input it directly into the CPU. This reduces the possibility of human error and is an economical means of data entry. Direct data entry devices include **magnetic stripe readers, chip readers and PIN pads, RFID readers, magnetic ink character readers (MICR), optical mark readers (OMR), optical character readers (OCR)** and **barcode readers**.

→ **Output devices** are any device that converts the electrical signals representing the results of processing, into a form that exists or can be sensed outside the computer. Output devices include the range of **monitors (CRT, TFT/LCD, IPS/LCD, LED)** and **touch screens** which are also input devices. Other output devices include **printers (laser, inkjet, dot matrix, wide format** and **3D), speakers, motors, buzzers, heaters** and **lamps/lights**.

SYLLABUS

This section will

- Detail the input devices and their uses, direct entry and associated devices and output devices and their uses.

2.1 Input devices and their uses

Input devices are hardware devices used to supply data and instructions to the computer for processing. A summary of each input device is shown here. Many of the examination questions on this topic focus on looking at the relative advantages and disadvantages of pairs of input devices.

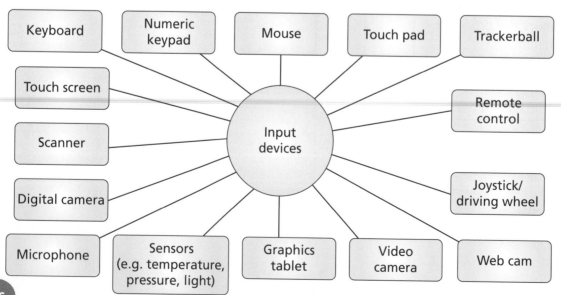

Keyboard entry	
Advantages	**Disadvantages**
No extra hardware to buy.	Slow method for entering large amounts of data.
Can visually verify the data on entry by looking at the screen.	Easy to make typing mistakes so error prone.
Can be used to issue instructions.	Hard for people with hand/arm disabilities to use.

Numeric keypad entry	
Advantages	**Disadvantages**
Small so takes up less space.	Small keys can be hard to see.
Portable so can be passed to customers to enable a PIN to be entered.	Some keys can be used to enter text as well as numbers, which can be confusing.

Using a mouse	
Advantages	**Disadvantages**
No extra hardware to buy if you have a desktop computer.	Can cause health problems (e.g. RSI).
Easier to make selections, move data, etc., compared to other methods.	Needs a flat surface which may not be available.
Can easily be configured for right- or left-handed users.	Hard for people with hand/arm disabilities to use.

Using a touch pad	
Advantages	**Disadvantages**
Can be used when there is no flat surface to use a mouse.	Can cause health problems (e.g. RSI).
No extra device to carry as the touch pad is built in.	Harder than a mouse for performing actions such as drag and drop.
Faster to navigate compared to keyboard use.	Hard for people with hand/arm disabilities to use.

Using a trackerball	
Advantages	**Disadvantages**
Easier to control than a mouse if you have limited hand/arm movement.	Cost as they have to be purchased separately.
Takes up less space than a conventional mouse.	Time is needed to get used to using them.

Using a remote control	
Advantages	**Disadvantages**
Can operate devices at a distance.	Signal is easily blocked by objects.
Batteries are needed, but the power consumption of remote controls is low, so batteries can last a long time.	Device is difficult to operate if the remote to it is lost.

Using a joystick	
Advantages	**Disadvantages**
They are ideal for quick movement.	They need to be purchased separately.
Can be operated by foot/mouth so can be used by disabled users.	Cannot be used easily for the entry of text (e.g. the name of the winners of games).

Using a touch screen	
Advantages	**Disadvantages**
No training is needed to use one as most people will have used one already.	Germs can be spread if lots of people use it.
Easier to use while standing, compared to a keyboard.	Icons are very small if the screen is small and this makes it hard to use.
Faster selection of options compared to using a keyboard.	Screen can get dirty, making it hard to see.

Using a scanner	
Advantages	**Disadvantages**
Can be used with OCR software to enter written text so that it can be entered into word-processing software for editing.	Scanners take up a large amount of space on the desk.
You can scan old photographs and improve/repair them using photo-editing software.	It can take time to scan a lot of documents.
Diagrams/pictures can be scanned at high resolution.	The scanned image can be poor if the resolution of the scanner is low.

Using a digital camera	
Advantages	**Disadvantages**
No film to develop so instant pictures.	Photographers need computer skills.
Digital images are easy to transfer.	Compression of images can cause loss in quality.
Large numbers of photographs can be taken and stored.	Some photographers say you get a better photograph using film.
Photos can be deleted to free up space. They are included with smartphones, which means you don't need to carry a separate camera.	Photos are so quick and simple to take that it is easy to amass a great number of photos which then need naming and archiving.

Using a microphone	
Advantages	**Disadvantages**
Safer as you can instruct without using hands (e.g. hands-free phone in a car).	Background noises can cause problems when using microphones for voice recognition.
You can use voice recognition to turn speech into text.	Voice recognition is not completely accurate so mistakes may occur.
You can input speech for VoIP which is a cheap way of making international phone calls using the internet.	Sound files take up a lot of disk space when stored.

Using sensors	
Advantages	**Disadvantages**
Readings are more accurate than those taken by humans.	Purchase cost.
Readings can be taken more frequently than by humans.	Dirt and grease may affect performance.
They work when a human is not present so cost less.	An ADC (analogue to digital converter) is needed to connect sensors to a computer as computers can process only digital data.

Using a graphics tablet	
Advantages	**Disadvantages**
Used in countries such as Japan and China where graphical characters are used instead of letters for words.	Specialist tablets are expensive.
More accurate to draw freehand on a tablet rather than using a mouse to draw.	Large size takes up space on the desk.
The icons/buttons are on the graphics tablet rather than the screen, leaving more space on the screen for the design/drawing.	

Using a web cam	
Advantages	**Disadvantages**
Can see the reactions of people as you are talking to them.	Limited extra features to improve image quality.
Parents can see their children and grandchildren and speak to them if they do not live near.	The picture quality can be poor at low resolution.
Can be used to conduct video-conferencing, which saves time and money travelling to meetings.	Generally have a fixed position so do not move around.

2.2 Direct data entry and associated devices

With direct data entry the data is contained on a machine-readable card or form so the data can be input directly into the computer by the input device. Direct data entry devices include magnetic stripe readers, chip and PIN readers, radio frequency identification (RFID) readers, magnetic ink character readers (MICR), optical mark readers and barcode readers.

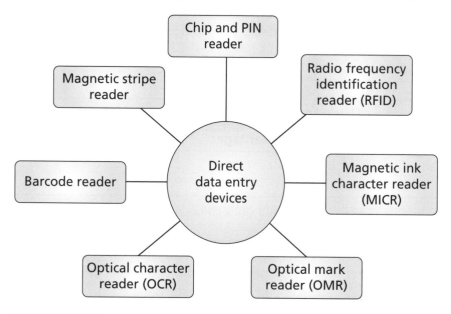

Using a magnetic stripe reader	
Advantages	**Disadvantages**
Faster input by swiping card rather than typing in details.	Stripes can be damaged by magnetic fields.
More accurate input of data compared to typing.	Stripes can store only a small amount of data.
Magnetic stripes are unaffected by water/moisture.	Stripes can wear with use.

Using a chip reader and PIN pad	
Advantages	**Disadvantages**
They have reduced fraud as the true cardholder has to input their PIN.	People sometimes forget their PIN.
Storage capacity for data on a chip is much higher than that for a magnetic stripe.	Other people can look when the PIN is being entered (called 'shoulder surfing').
Chips are harder to copy compared to a magnetic stripe.	Not all countries can use chip and PIN, so they have to use magnetic stripe readers.
Chips are less likely to be damaged compared to a magnetic stripe.	

Using an RFID reader	
Advantages	**Disadvantages**
Tags can be read at a distance.	The readers and tags are expensive.
Compared to barcodes tags store more data.	Harder to copy compared to a magnetic stripe which reduces fraud.
RFID systems can scan multiple items simultaneously.	Because the tags can be read at a distance some people are worried that others could access the information.

Using a magnetic ink character reader	
Advantages	**Disadvantages**
Cheque details are read with 100% accuracy.	The equipment is very expensive.
Difficult to forge.	The cheque's value needs to be input using a keyboard, which is slow.
Cheques can be read even if they have been folded.	
Cheques can be read at very high speed.	

2.3 Output devices and their uses

Output devices convert the electrical signals representing the results of processing, into a form that exists or can be sensed outside the computer. The main output devices are monitors/screens, printers and speakers but the output signals from a computer can be used to switch devices on/off such as heaters, lamps/lights, motors, etc., in control systems.

Monitors/screens are any display device on which information can be shown. The main types are:

CRT monitors – large, heavy old-fashioned monitors that are not energy efficient.

TFT/LCD (thin film transistor/liquid crystal display) monitors – thin screens and low power monitors which are replacing CRT monitors because they are smaller and lighter but they have the disadvantage of a narrow viewing angle. These monitors give off less radiation compared to a CRT monitor.

IPS (in-plane switching)/LCD screens have a wider viewing angle compared to TFT/LCD and the colour reproduction is better but they do have higher power consumption and are more expensive.

LED screens use very little power and produce higher quality images compared to ordinary LCD screens.

Touch screens are both input and output devices and users are able to alter what they see on the screen.

Multimedia projectors project the image onto a much larger screen so that an audience is able to view the output.

Printers

The following printers are available:

Laser printer – use toner cartridges and are fast printers ideal for office work.

Inkjet printer – use ink cartridges and are good for printing in colour. They are generally more popular for home use. They are cheap to buy but expensive to run as the ink cartridges are expensive. They are also slow and the ink can smudge when wet.

Dot matrix printer – uses little pins which hit an inked ribbon to form dots which make up the shape of a letter. They are slow and noisy but can be useful as they use continuous stationery and can print on multi-part stationery.

Wide format printer – use either laser or inkjet technology and are used where the width of the paper is large.

3D printer – a printer that lays down layers of material (e.g. plastic, metal, ceramic) to form a three-dimensional product.

Advantages and disadvantages of different types of printer

Laser printer	
Advantages	**Disadvantages**
Quiet so can be used in offices where phones are used.	More expensive to buy.
Toner cartridges last longer than inkjet cartridges.	Can be larger than other printers so take up more space.
High printing speed.	High power consumption.
No wet pages with ink that smudges.	Colour lasers are very expensive.
Lower cost per page to print compared to inkjet.	

Inkjet printer	
Advantages	**Disadvantages**
Usually takes up less space than a laser printer.	Ink cartridges do not last long and so need regular replacement.
Low initial purchase cost.	Cost more per page than laser printers.
High quality photographs can be printed.	Slower print speed.
They do not produce ozone like laser printers which could cause health problems.	Wet ink on the pages can smudge.

Dot matrix printer	
Advantages	**Disadvantages**
Usually takes up less space than a laser printer.	Very noisy so hard to use a phone if the printer is printing.
Can be used with continuous stationery.	Very low quality print (e.g. appears dotty).
Cheaper to run than inkjet printers.	Unsuitable for printing graphics.

Wide format printers

Used for wide printouts (e.g. maps, posters and plans) and can use laser or inkjet technology and are expensive specialist printers.

3D printers

Use an additive technique where layers of a substance (usually plastic, glass, ceramic or metal) is repeatedly sprayed in layers to build up the 3D effect.

Uses include:

- Dentistry for producing crowns, bridges, veneers and false teeth that are designed using computer-aided design software and printed using a 3D printer.
- For producing prosthetic limbs that fit the patient perfectly.
- For producing hearing aids that fit a patient's ear perfectly.
- For producing quick prototypes of products (e.g. the body design of a new car).

Exam preparation

1 A Give the names of the following input/output devices:

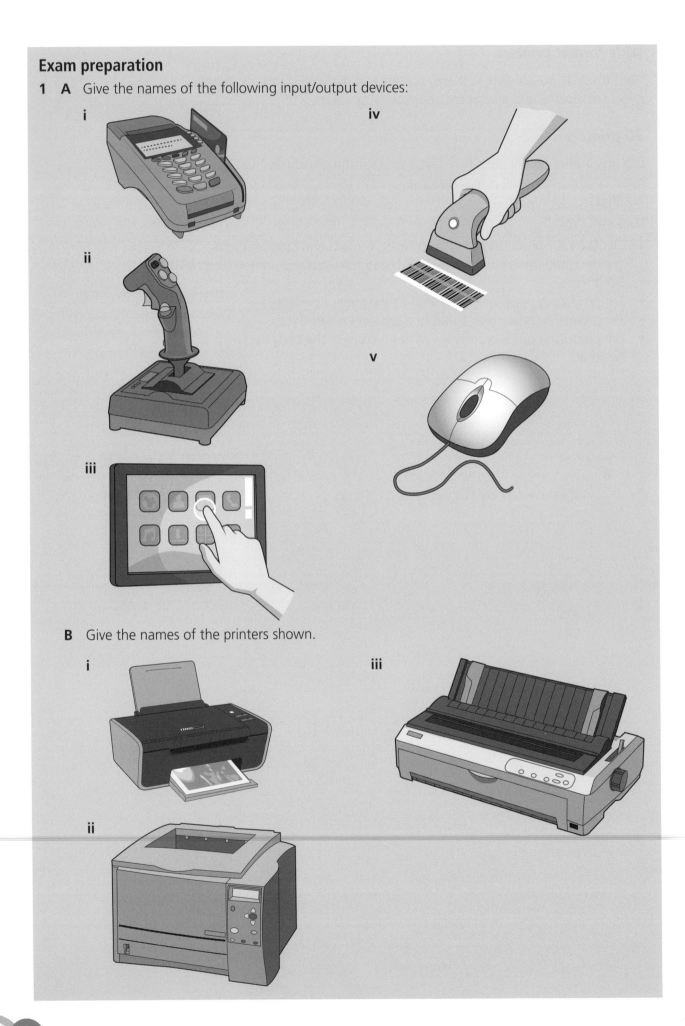

i

ii

iii

iv

v

B Give the names of the printers shown.

i

ii

iii

Exam-style questions

1   Tick true or false next to each of these statements.

	true	false
Dot matrix printers produce high quality output.		
Inkjet printers are a lot noisier than dot matrix printers.		
Wide format printers are used when very large hard copy is needed.		
Inkjet printers always use continuous stationery.		
Laser printers are usually much faster than inkjet printers.		

2   Give **two** advantages and **two** disadvantages of using RFID as a method of inputting data.

3   Optical character readers and optical mark readers are examples of direct data entry devices.
    A   Explain what is meant by a direct data entry device.
    B   Give the names of **two** direct data entry devices other than optical mark readers.

Important things to remember

Fill in the missing key words

Input devices are used to enter data and _____ into the computer for processing. _____ come with most computers and can be physical or on-screen. Pointing devices are used to make selections using a GUI and these can be mice or _____. _____, which are like upside down mice, can also be used to make selections.

Numeric keypads are smaller than ordinary keyboards and usually just contain numbers and are used with chip and _____ for entering personal identification numbers when using a credit/debit card.

Other input devices include _____ controls for controlling devices such as TVs at a distance and _____ for playing computer games.

A _____ _____ is an input device that detects the presence and location when a screen is touched and is found with tablet computers and smartphones.

Larger input devices include _____ which can be used to digitise documents and old photographs. When used with special _____ software, it is possible for the scanned text to be recognised as individual letters so that they can be input into a word-processed document. _____ cameras are input devices and can be bought separately or combined in tablet computers and smartphones and the images are easily stored in the cloud for access from any device with internet access. _____ are input devices that allow speech to be recorded, or for verbal instructions to be given to the operating system to accomplish tasks. Such systems use voice _____ and are fairly accurate provided the person speaks clearly and there is no background noise.

_____ such as those measuring pressure, temperature, light and humidity/moisture are used to input signals in control systems. In these systems, the processor decides what action should be taken by the _____ devices.

Video cameras are _____ devices that capture both still and moving images and are now built into tablet computers and smartphones.

_____ _____ can be used to input live video images and this in conjunction with a microphone allows you to conduct conversations using the internet where you can see the person you are talking to.

There is a range of input devices called _____ data entry devices where data is input directly from a form or a card into the computer for processing. Direct data entry devices include _____ stripe readers, chip readers and _____ pads, RFID readers, magnetic _____ _____ readers, optical _____ readers, barcode readers and _____ character readers.

Screens/monitors are the most popular _____ device as they are part of every computer system or smartphone. _____ monitors are the large, heavy and now old-fashioned monitors that have been replaced by the thin and lighter _____ screens that are used with most desktop and laptop computers. The _____ given off by an LCD screen is much less than that produced by a CRT monitor and the heat given off is also much less. In-plane switching, or _____ for short, is a type of LCD screen which has a faster response time to fast-moving images and where there is a greater viewing angle allowing more people to view the screen at the same time.

Another type of monitor is the _____ monitor which is very light compared to CRT monitors and uses much less power which is why they are used in portable devices which are powered by rechargeable batteries.

If the output from the screen needs to be viewed by a lot of people then a _____ projector can be used to project the image from a computer onto a large screen. When projected onto a large screen the image _____ is not as good and the projector needs to be used in a darkened room.

Speakers and headphones/earphones are _____ devices used to output speech/sounds and music. Output devices used as output from _____ systems include motors, buzzers, lamps and heaters.

10 MINUTE TEST

1 Tick true or false next to each of these statements.

	true	false
A laser printer and a motor are both examples of output devices.		
Sensors are output devices.		
A pressure sensor is used to send data to a processor in a washing machine.		
A dot matrix printer uses continuous stationery.		
Speakers are input devices.		

2 Tick true or false next to each of these statements.

	true	false
A touch screen is both an input and output device.		
A wide format printer is used to print large maps and plans.		
An inkjet printer is usually noisier than a dot matrix printer.		
OMR can be used to read data from multiple-choice answer sheets.		
OCR is used to read the data on bank cheques.		

3 This question is about choice of printers. The following printers are available.

Dot matrix printer
Inkjet printer
Wide format printer
3D printer

Choose the most appropriate printer from the above list for each of the following tasks:

A For printing out long stock lists on continuous stationery in a warehouse.
B For printing out a poster on paper which is 60 cm (about 24 inches) wide advertising a school play.
C Printing false teeth to replace a patient's missing teeth.
D Producing a printout on multi-part stationery where the copies are sent to different departments in a company.
E For printing the large plan of a new shopping centre.
F For home use printing out copies of photographs to show to a friend.
G For printing the prototype of a new car body that has been designed using computer-aided design software (CAD).

4 Some items of data can be input into a computer using direct data entry. Write down the name of the most appropriate input devices used to enter each of these items of data.

A Data about a customer stored on a magnetic stripe on a store loyalty card.
B Marks on the answer sheet for a multiple-choice examination paper.
C Used to input the details about a person on a tag in a passport, so that it can be decided whether they should be allowed access to a country at Border Control.
D Data contained in magnetic ink at the bottom of a bank cheque.

5 Describe **two** types of medical aid that can be printed using a 3D printer.

6 A library is planning to replace the barcodes on its books with RFID tags.

Describe **two** advantages and **two** disadvantages in the library using RFID tags rather than barcodes for inputting book and borrower details.

3 Storage devices and media

REVISION SUMMARY

→ **Storage devices** are those devices such as fixed hard disk drives that read/write data from or onto the storage media. **Internal memory** (RAM and ROM) is fast but expensive and RAM loses its contents when the power is removed so more permanent storage is needed and this is why we have storage devices.

→ Storage devices are used to hold data and instructions that are not needed immediately for processing by the computer. **Magnetic backing storage media** includes **fixed hard disks** which are internal hardware (i.e. inside the casing of the computer) and **portable hard disks** which are external hardware devices (i.e. outside the casing of the computer) that can be easily transported from one computer to another.

→ **Magnetic tapes** are storage media that have a large storage capacity and are used mainly for backing up the data stored on a fixed hard disk.

→ **Optical media** such as **CD ROM**, **DVD ROM** from which data can be read, but a user cannot store data on them. They are used mainly for the distribution of software. DVD ROM has a higher storage capacity than CD ROM and is used for the distribution of films.

→ **CD R** and **DVD R** both allow a user to record data onto the media but only once, so they are useful for archiving files. **CD RW** allows a user to write data many times to the CD. **DVD RW** also allows data to be written to the disk many times but the storage capacity is much higher than CD RW.

→ **Solid state backing storage** includes **pen drives/memory sticks/USB sticks/flash drives** which are ideal for backups of small amounts of data and memory cards which are mainly used for storing image files in digital cameras. Solid state backing storage is storage on chips so there are no moving parts, which makes it more durable.

SYLLABUS

This section will

- Detail storage devices, their associated media and their uses, and describe their advantages and disadvantages.

3.1 Storage devices and media

Backing storage is storage other than ROM or RAM that is non-volatile (i.e. does not lose its contents when the power is removed) and is used to hold programs and data not being used.

Backing storage devices are the hardware devices that enable data to be written to and read from the storage media, on which the data and programs are stored.

Magnetic backing storage media

Fixed hard disks, portable hard disks and magnetic tape all store data as a magnetic pattern on the surface of a disk or tape. The drive is the hardware that does the reading/writing of the data onto the media which are magnetic disk or tape. Hard disks have high access speeds so data can be found and read quickly, a high transfer rate so data can be written to the disk quickly, and a high storage capacity.

Magnetic tape stores data on plastic tape with a magnetic coating on a reel or cartridge. It is ideal for backing up hard disks where all the data on the disk needs to be copied, such as on a server. Because magnetic tape is removable, it can be moved to a safe place. It is not suitable for uses where a particular item of data needs to be read off the tape as it would take too long to find. The access speed is therefore low.

Magnetic tape has a much higher storage capacity than a hard disk and the speed at which data can be copied is high and it is mainly used for making backups of data.

Optical backing storage media

Optical backing storage devices store data as a series of small bumps on a plastic disk acting as the storage media. There are a variety of storage media, some of which can only read the data, some of which can read and write the data only once onto the disk, and some of which can read and write the data many times.

Here is a brief summary of the different types of optical backing storage media:

CD ROM (compact disk read-only memory) – data is read-only so the user cannot store their own data on the disk. Ideal for distribution of small programs and music.

DVD ROM (digital versatile disk read-only memory) stores more data than CD ROM, and like CD ROM it is read-only. Ideal for the distribution of large programs and films.

CD R or **DVD R** (the R means recordable) – user can record data onto the disk but only once. Good for storing downloaded files or other files as a backup.

CD RW (the RW means rewritable) – allows the recording and re-use of CDs by a user so data stored can be updated.

DVD RW (the RW means rewritable) – allows the recording and re-use of DVDs by a user so the data stored can be updated.

DVD RAM (digital versatile disk random access memory) – like DVD RW you can save your own data and update it but it is much faster and easier to overwrite the data.

Blu-ray – higher storage capacity disk compared to DVD and is used to store high definition films/video but can be used to store other data.

Solid state backing storage – has no moving parts and is small. It can store the data when the power is removed but the storage capacity is smaller than that of a portable hard disk. Memory sticks/pen drives/ flash drives/USB sticks and flash memory cards are all examples of solid state backing storage. Uses for flash memory cards include storage of photographs in digital cameras, and memory sticks/pen drives can be used to transfer files between computers.

Backups

Backups are copies of data and programs kept for security purposes in case the originals become damaged or lost. Backup copies must be taken on removable media so they can be moved to a safe place (usually off-site). Portable hard disk, magnetic tape, writable optical media and solid state storage devices are all suitable for taking backups.

3.2 The advantages and disadvantages of the different storage devices

You are often asked to make comparisons between different storage devices/media. Here are tables showing the advantages/disadvantages of different devices/media.

Fixed hard disk	
Advantages	**Disadvantages**
High access speed (i.e. finding and reading data).	Not removable like a portable hard disk so no use for transferring files between computers.
High transfer rate when writing data.	Cannot be removed and locked away for security purposes.
High storage capacity. Usually higher than optical disks or solid state memory but not as high as magnetic tape.	

Portable hard disk	
Advantages	**Disadvantages**
High access speed (i.e. finding and reading data).	Small size means they are easily lost or stolen.
High transfer rate when writing data.	Easy for confidential data to be copied to them.
High storage capacity like fixed hard disk.	Movement between computers means they can spread viruses.
Easy to attach to any computer with a USB port.	

Magnetic tape	
Advantages	**Disadvantages**
Extremely high storage capacity makes them ideal media for backups.	Not good for storage where access to different data items is required as access is very slow.
Less expensive than similar storage capacity portable hard disks.	Cannot update details on the tape without creating a whole new tape.
Data transfer rate is high, which makes it fast for taking backups.	

CD RW	
Advantages	**Disadvantages**
User can write their own data onto the disk.	Since it is optical media it is easily damaged.
Data stored on the disk can be altered.	Data transfer rate is lower than hard disk.
Disks are cheap to purchase.	Not all computers have an optical drive to read/write the disk.

CD ROM or DVD ROM	
Advantages	**Disadvantages**
Data cannot be erased off the disk by the user.	You cannot store your own data on the disk as it is read-only.
Can be used to distribute software packages.	Since it is optical media it is easily damaged.
Blank disks are cheap to purchase.	Data transfer rate is lower than hard disk.
	Not all computers have an optical drive to read disk.

DVD RAM	
Advantages	**Disadvantages**
Faster access to data compared to DVD R or DVD RW.	The devices to read/write data are more expensive than other optical devices.
Faster transfer rate compared to DVD R or DVD RW.	Disks are more expensive than other optical media.
Some disks are in cartridges which makes them less susceptible to damage compared to other optical disks.	Takes longer to write to the disk compared to other writable disk drives.

Blu-ray	
Advantages	**Disadvantages**
Higher storage capacity compared to other optical disks enables HD films to be stored.	Disks on which a user can store their data are expensive compared to other optical media.
Faster transfer rate compared to DVD R or DVD RW.	Need a drive capable of reading Blu-ray disks.
Can play back video and record simultaneously.	

Solid state backing storage	
Advantages	**Disadvantages**
No moving parts so less easily damaged.	Lower storage capacity compared to hard disks.
Can be used in any device with a USB port or memory card slot.	Cannot repair if damaged.
Silent in operation.	Small so easily lost or stolen.
Small so easily portable.	Lower access speed compared to a hard disk.
Cannot be scratched like optical media.	

Exam preparation

1 Use the information contained in the tables in Section 3.2 (advantages and disadvantages of the different storage devices), page 31, to compare advantages and disadvantages of:

A Fixed hard disk compared to optical disk.

B Portable hard disk compared to a pen drive (i.e. a type of solid state memory).

C Fixed hard disk compared to magnetic tape.

Exam-style question

1 Desktop computers and smartphones can be used to access the internet.

A Give **two** advantages in using a desktop computer rather than a smartphone for this purpose.

B Give **two** disadvantages in using a desktop computer rather than a smartphone for this purpose.

Important things to remember

Fill in the missing key words

The material on which data and programs are stored is called the storage _____ and the device doing the recording is called the storage _____. Backing storage is not as fast as internal memory but it is cheaper, and unlike RAM, it does not lose its contents when there is no power. Backing storage is defined as storage other than _____ and RAM which is non-volatile and is used to hold _____ not being used.

Magnetic storage media stores data as a _____ pattern on the storage media which is usually hard disk or _____.
Hard disks have a high _____ speed, a high transfer rate and a very high _____ capacity. _____ hard disks cannot be removed from the computer whereas _____ hard disks can be.

Magnetic tapes have a huge storage capacity and are ideal for backing up data stored on large hard disks such as those used as _____ for networks. They are suitable when all the data and programs on the hard disk need to be _____ but are unsuitable when _____ access to data is needed.

_____ disks store data as a series of bumps on a plastic disk which reflect laser light. CD ROM is _____-only and is used to store programs and music. DVD ROM is also read-only and has a larger _____ capacity compared to CD ROM and is used to store movies. CD R and DVD R can have data _____ onto them but only once but _____ allows the CD to have data recorded onto them by the user many times. DVD RW drives can be used to read as well as _____ data and the newer DVD RAM are much faster at reading and writing data.

Blu-ray disks have a higher storage capacity than those mentioned previously and are used for the storage of movies in _____ definition.

Solid _____ backing storage devices have no moving parts and are small and reliable, although their storage capacities are _____. They have lower _____ speeds compared to hard disks and are small so they are easily lost or stolen. They include _____ cards and memory sticks or _____ drives and are ideal for transferring small files between computers.

10 MINUTE TEST

1 List **four** items from the following which are storage devices.

Magnetic ink character reader

Memory stick   Laser printer

Magnetic tape drive   RFID reader

Portable hard disk drive   Touch screen

DVD RAM drive   3D printer

CRT monitor   Scanner

2 Tick true or false next to each of these statements.

	true	false
Magnetic hard disk drives are always portable.		
An optical disk which can have data updated is DVD RW.		
Fixed hard disks are unsuitable for taking backup copies.		
Solid state backing storage includes magnetic tape.		
Blu-ray disks have a larger storage capacity than DVD.		

3 A doctor's surgery uses a computer network for storing and accessing patient records. One of the doctors is worried about losing the data and is investigating the various methods of backing up data stored on the server.

A Explain what is meant by a backup.

B The doctor has decided to use either a portable magnetic hard disk or magnetic tape to create backups.

   i Explain why **both** media must be removable from the drives used to read/write the data.

   ii Discuss the advantages and disadvantages of using each of these media.

4 Tick true or false next to each of these statements.

	true	false
Fixed hard disk and portable hard disk are both examples of magnetic media.		
Memory cards are examples of magnetic media.		
Memory cards are thin cards used mainly in cameras for storing photographs.		
Memory cards cannot be removed from the camera.		
Magnetic tape can be used for taking backup copies of data stored on servers.		

5 Two types of backing storage suitable for taking backup copies of programs and data are portable hard disk and solid state backing storage.

A Describe why each of these is suitable for taking backups.

B Describe **one** difference between portable hard disk and solid state backing storage.

C Flash memory cards are a type of solid state backing storage.

   i Give the name of another type of solid state backing storage.

   ii Give **one** use for the solid state backing storage you have described in part **i**.

4 Networks and the effects of using them

REVISION SUMMARY

→ A **network** is two or more computers linked together so that they are able to share resources such as printers, scanners, software, an internet connection and data.

→ **Network devices** are needed to build a network. These include routers, which can be used to join networks together such as a small home network and the internet. **Routers** inspect packets of data for the address and then forward the packet on to the next network and so on.

→ **Network interface cards** are needed to make a cable connection between a computer and the network. **Hubs** and **switches** are used to join computers and other devices to form a network. **Bridges** are used to connect small local area networks together to form a larger network.

→ **Modems**, like routers, can provide an internet connection.

→ **Wireless communication** between devices can be using WiFi or Bluetooth. WiFi has a greater range compared to Bluetooth.

→ **Web browser software** is used to view web pages stored on the internet. To access the internet you can use a permanent connection which is very expensive or alternatively you can use an internet service provider (ISP).

→ The **internet** is a huge network of networks that enable communication using email, instant messaging and VoIP. You can also search for information and access websites for e-commerce.

→ The world wide web (**www**) is a way of storing and accessing the information on web pages stored on the internet.

→ **Intranets** are private networks that make use of internet technology and only people who are allowed access to the information can access it.

→ There are two types of network: A **LAN** (**local area network**) and a **WAN** (**wide area network**). A LAN can be wired or wireless in which case it is called a **WLAN** (**wireless local area network**).

SYLLABUS

This section will:

• Detail the purpose of a router and how it works.

• Detail common network devices such as network interface cards, hubs, bridges, switches and modems.

• Detail the use of WiFi and Bluetooth and how to set up and configure a small network.

• Detail the characteristics and purpose of common network environments such as intranets and the internet.

• Detail the advantages and disadvantages of using different types of computer to access the internet.

• Detail the security issues regarding data transfer and different network communications (i.e. fax, email, audio-conferencing, web-conferencing).

4.1 Network devices

To create a network you need certain devices.

A network interface card – these are already fitted in most computers and connect straight to the motherboard and provide an external socket to which the network cable can be connected.

A hub – is used to connect computers and other devices such as printers and scanners to the network. Data is transferred through the network in packets and the hub transmits the packets of data to all the computers and devices on the network, whether the data is intended for the computers or devices or not. A hub therefore does not manage the data passing through it.

A switch – is like a hub in that it is used to connect computers and devices on the network. It is more intelligent as it inspects the packets of data so that they are not forwarded to every device but instead are sent only to the computer/device the packet is intended for. This reduces network traffic.

A router – reads the address on a packet of data and directs the packet on to the next network on its journey to its destination. Other routers on other networks will do the same until the packet reaches its final destination. They can be used to join several wired or wireless networks together. They can also be used to connect a LAN to a WAN.

A bridge – is used to divide a larger network into smaller LANs. Only data which needs to pass from one LAN to another will cross over the bridge thus reducing network traffic. A bridge has only two ports to connect one LAN to another.

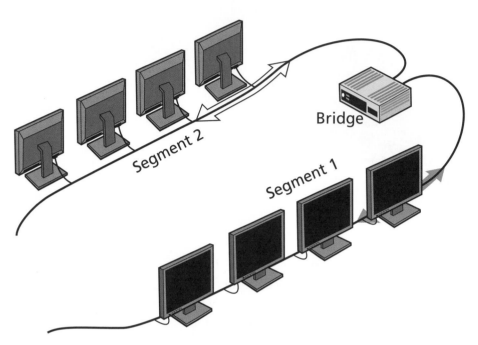

If a computer in segment 1 needs to send data to a computer in segment 1 then no data will pass over the bridge. This will reduce the data travelling in segment 2. If a computer in segment 1 needs to send data to a computer in segment 2 then the data will be allowed to cross the bridge.

A modem – turns a digital signal from a computer into an analogue (i.e. sound) signal that can pass along a telephone line. A modem at the other end of the line turns the analogue signal back to a digital signal so it can be understood by the computer. Modems were mainly used to connect to the internet but now most people use routers for this purpose.

Modems such as this have been largely replace by routers as a method of providing an internet connection.

WiFi and Bluetooth

WiFi and Bluetooth are both used for communication between computers/ devices using radio waves.

WiFi is used to provide internet access in homes and public places. Provided you are in range of the wireless router you can access the internet. There are no trailing wires or network wires to install. The range of a WiFi signal depends on the strength of the router and also if there are any obstacles in the way of the signal.

Bluetooth is used to exchange data over short distances compared to WiFi. For example, you can play music from your smartphone in your car without the need for any cables. Bluetooth is also used in hands-free headsets for smartphones.

Setting up and configuring a small network

The steps are as follows:

1   Pay a subscription to an internet service provider (ISP) to supply an internet connection. The ISP will also provide storage on their server for your own website, email facilities, access to online shopping and services such as news, weather, sport, etc.
2   Connect the router to the cable point or telephone line.
3   Connect any cabled devices/computers to the router using cables.
4   Connect any wireless devices to the router using the passcode.
5   Install web browser software on any computers that need to access the internet (if one is not already installed) which will let you obtain information by entering web addresses (URLs), using internet portals, using key word searches, using links and using menus.

4.2 Network issues and communication

The **internet** is the largest network in the world and when you connect to the internet your computer/network is added to the huge network.

The internet	
Advantages	**Disadvantages**
Provides lots of communication methods (e.g. email, text messaging, social media, etc.).	Misinformation: anybody can create a website containing false information.
Access to a huge store of information on the world wide web.	Some websites are fake and are used to collect personal details such as credit card details which are then used to commit fraud.
Enables online shopping, banking, etc.	Social networking sites, chat rooms, etc., present an e-safety danger for young people.

Intranets – are private networks used usually within an organisation which use internet technology such as web pages and browsers for their operation. Sometimes people from outside the organisation are allowed access in which case they have to enter a user-ID and password in order to gain access to the network.

Local area networks (LANs) and wide area networks (WANs)

LANs are small networks usually confined to a single site or building and the organisation that uses the LAN also owns the communication equipment. A WAN is a much larger network covering a wide geographical area and the communication equipment is owned by a third party.

LAN (local area network)	WAN (wide area network)
Confined to a small area.	Covers a wide geographical area (e.g. between cities, countries and even continents).
Usually located in a single building.	In lots of different buildings and cities, countries, etc.
Uses cable, wireless and microwave links which are usually owned by the organisation.	Uses more expensive telecommunication links that are supplied by telecommunication companies (e.g. satellite links).

WLANs (Wireless local area network) and cabled LANs (Local area networks)

LANs use cables whereas WLANs use wireless technology to send/receive data between computers/devices.

WLAN compared to a cabled LAN	
Advantages	Disadvantages
Fewer cables to buy, so cheaper.	Obstacles interfere with the signal.
Easier to connect devices (e.g. printer, scanner).	Slower data transmission rates.
Can work anywhere in range of the signal.	Limited area in which to work.
	Easier to hack into so less secure.

The advantages and disadvantages of using different types of computer to access the internet

Many different devices can be used to access the internet and each has its own advantages and disadvantages and these are summarised in the following tables:

Using a smartphone to access the internet	
Advantages	Disadvantages
Can access the internet anywhere there is WiFi or a mobile signal.	Not easy for parents to police.
You can stay connected while moving around.	Trimmed down websites used with smartphones may not give the information required.
Device is very portable and you are likely to have access to it more than other computers.	Small screen and keyboard are hard to use.

Using a tablet to access the internet	
Advantages	**Disadvantages**
Lighter and more portable than laptops and desktops.	Smaller screen compared to laptops and desktops can make them harder to use.
Larger screens compared to smartphones make them easier to use.	On-screen keyboard is more difficult to use compared to the keyboard on a laptop or desktop.
Easier to use when standing up compared to a laptop or desktop.	When used in an awkward position, may lead to health problems.

Using a laptop to access the internet	
Advantages	**Disadvantages**
Portable compared to a desktop computer.	Not as portable as a smartphone or tablet because of its size and weight.
Almost full-sized keyboard is easier to use compared to those on a tablet or smartphone.	Screen and keyboard are attached and this can lead to backache.
Fairly large screen makes reading web pages easier.	Touch pads are harder to use compared to a mouse when there is no flat surface available.
Can be used when a flat surface is not available.	

Using a desktop computer to access the internet	
Advantages	**Disadvantages**
Full-sized keyboard and mouse are easier to use.	Large and heavy so not portable.
You can view the full versions of a website rather than trimmed down versions for tablets or smartphones.	Hard to use while standing up.
Screen and keyboard are adjustable so there are fewer health problems.	Occupies the most amount of desk space.
Large screen means text is easier to read.	

Security issues regarding data transfer

When computers are networked the security problems increase and here are some of the main issues:

Password interception – once other people find out your password they can log on to the internet as you, read your emails, and find out other personal and financial information.

Virus attack – a virus is a program that copies itself automatically, causes deletion of programs/data or annoyance and can make computers run slowly and crash. The following steps can be taken to prevent a virus attack:

- Install antivirus software.
- Perform scans of all media on a regular basis.
- Keep the antivirus software up-to-date because new viruses are being created all the time.

- Do not download any programs from sites unless the sites are trusted or well-known.
- Do not open file attachments to emails unless they are from a trusted source.
- Any removable media such as pen drives and portable hard disks should be scanned for viruses before use.

Hackers accessing the network – hackers will try to guess a password or use a cracking program which will try millions of passwords in turn. Sometimes key logging software (i.e. spyware) is put on a user's computer to record their keystrokes and obtain their passwords.

Firewalls – hardware, software or both that looks at data being sent to and from a network to check whether or not it should be allowed through the firewall. It can also alert a user if a program is being run on their computer without their permission.

User-IDs and passwords – user-IDs identify a user to the network, and a password is used to check that the person accessing the network is genuine. Strong passwords that are hard to crack by hackers should be used and these should include a combination of letters (capitals and lower case), numbers and symbols.

Biometric authentication techniques

Biometric authentication techniques use a unique property of the human body to recognise that the user is the correct person to be allowed access to the network.

Biometric authentication techniques include:

- **Fingerprinting** – uses the unique pattern on a person's finger to decide whether or not access to the network should be given.
- **Iris scanning** – uses the unique pattern on the coloured area of the eye surrounding the pupil to decide whether or not access should be given.
- **Retinal scanning** – uses the unique pattern of blood vessels at the back of the eye to decide whether or not to give access.

Encryption

Encryption is the process of scrambling personal data such as credit card details, banking details, confidential emails, etc., before sending over a network. If a hacker intercepts the data, then it will not make sense to them as it will be scrambled. The receiving computer will descramble the data so that it can be understood by the recipient. This process requires an encryption and decryption key.

Data protection laws

Many countries have data protection laws which protect their people against misuse of personal data. Personal data is data about a person who is living and is more personal than just their name and address. Personal data would include date of birth, medical records, credit history, salary, employment history, etc.

Wrong personal data could result in wrong medical treatment, not being given a job, being refused a loan, etc.

A data protection law will usually ask organisations that hold personal data to register their use and it will also allow the person the data is about to view the data and have it corrected if it is wrong.

Most data protection includes data protection principles such as:

- Personal data must be processed fairly and lawfully.
- Personal data should be adequate, relevant and not excessive.
- Personal data should be accurate and kept up-to-date.
- Measures should be taken to protect the personal data held from unauthorised access, theft or destruction.
- Personal data should not be transferred to another country that does not have adequate data protection laws.

Network communication

Networks offer different methods of communication including the following:

Physical fax – are the fax machines connected to a phone line. The fax scans a document and then sends the data as a series of sounds down a telephone line where the fax at the other end converts it back to an image which is then printed out.

Electronic/internet fax – internet technology is used and the fax is saved on a computer so it can be read and printed out if necessary.

The main differences between the two methods are summarised here:

Physical fax	Electronic/internet fax
No computer network is used.	A computer network is used.
A dedicated phone line for the fax is needed.	No additional phone line is needed.
Faxes are always printed which can waste paper.	You can view the fax and print only the ones you want.
Need to purchase a physical fax machine.	A computer is needed which you are likely to have already.
Cannot send faxes from mobile devices.	Can send faxes from mobile devices.
Need to buy ink and paper.	Reduced ink and paper requirements.
Only one fax can be sent or received at the same time.	Can send and receive multiple faxes at the same time.
Need to pay for a phone call to send a fax.	No cost of a phone call.

Email

Emails are electronic messages sent from one communication device to another. Files can be attached to emails as file attachments. There are a number of advantages and disadvantages of using email compared to physical faxing and these are summarised in the table at the top of page 42.

Email compared to fax	
Advantages	**Disadvantages**
Emails can be viewed without others seeing them as faxes are usually printed out in an area shared by other employees.	Emails can be used to distribute viruses. Faxes do not spread viruses.
Emails can be viewed on any portable device (computer, smartphone, etc.) with internet access. Physical faxes are received only by using a fax machine.	Faxed signed documents are usually legally acceptable whereas emails are not.
The information in fax form is not normally a computer file and cannot be edited by the receiver.	
The receiver's fax machine may be out of paper and this will prevent the fax from being received. With emails this problem does not arise.	
Cheaper to use email. Sending a physical fax means you have to pay for the cost of the phone call as well as the cost of the paper and ink.	

Conferencing systems

There are a number of ways of communicating with groups of people and these are:

Video-conferencing – two or more individuals in different places can talk and see each other in real time and also exchange electronic documents. The hardware needed includes a video compression card, a sound card, a microphone, a web cam and specialist software.

Web-conferencing – conferencing events can be shared with an audience in remote locations. There is usually one sender and many recipients so it is ideal for training events, meetings, lectures and presentations.

Audio-conferencing – only uses voice to conduct a meeting between a few people. Sometimes this is called a conference call.

Video-conferencing	
Advantages	**Disadvantages**
Less stress as employees do not have to experience delays at airports, accidents, road works, etc.	The initial cost of the equipment, as specialist video-conferencing equipment is expensive.
Improved family life, as less time spent away from home staying in hotels.	Poor image and sound quality.
Saves travelling time.	People can feel very self-conscious when using video-conferencing and not communicate effectively.
More environmentally friendly as there are fewer people travelling to meetings. This cuts down on carbon dioxide emissions.	

Video-conferencing (continued)	
Advantages	**Disadvantages**
Saves money as the company doesn't have to spend money on travelling expenses, hotel rooms, meals, etc.	Although documents and diagrams in digital form can be passed around, an actual product or component cannot be passed around.
Improved productivity of employees, as they are not wasting time travelling.	Lack of face-to-face contact may mean a discussion may not be as effective.
Meetings can be called at very short notice without too much planning.	If the delegates are in distant locations, the picture can be out of synchronisation with the speech, which can be distracting.

Policing the internet

Some people think that the internet should be policed. Here are some of the arguments for and against.

Yes, the internet should be policed:

- It is too easy for children to access undesirable content.
- Other media such as TV, films and advertising are regulated so the internet should be policed as well.
- Misinformation about a person can ruin their reputation/life.
- Too many sites promoting drugs, violence, etc.
- People can hide through the anonymity of the internet.

No, the internet should not be policed:

- It would take resources no law enforcement agency would have.
- Free speech is a fundamental right and should not be removed.
- What is allowable in one country is *not* allowable in another country, which would make the internet very difficult to police.
- It should be up to individuals to decide whether or not they wish to view certain content.

Exam preparation

1 Describe **three** methods that can be used to help prevent hackers gaining illegal access to a computer network.

Exam-style question

1 Desktop computers and smartphones can be used to access the internet.

A Give **two** advantages in using a desktop computer rather than a smartphone for this purpose.

B Give **two** disadvantages in using a desktop computer rather than a smartphone for this purpose.

Important things to remember

Fill in the missing key words

_____ are two or more computers linked together so that they can share resources such as printers, an internet connection, software and data. _____ devices are needed to build a network and these can include _____ that read address information to determine the final destination of packets of data and can connect networks so they are able to share a single _____ connection. Network _____ cards are needed which connect the motherboard to an external socket into which network cables can be connected. _____ and switches are used to connect devices in a network but a switch is more intelligent as it _____ packets of data to check they are being forwarded to the correct computer.

There are other network devices such as _____ used to connect local area networks together and _____ which convert digital data into sound and vice versa so that telephone lines can be used to transmit data.

Wireless communication between computers and other devices can be achieved using _____ or WiFi and the former is used over _____ distances and where slow bandwidth is acceptable.

Once the computers and other network devices have been connected or linked you need an _____ to provide you with an internet connection as to have one yourself is very _____.

You then need _____ software to allow web pages stored on the internet to be viewed. The internet is a huge _____ of networks and the _____ is a way of accessing the information on these networked computers.

Internal networks can also make use of internet technology and these are called _____. These networks hold information that is used by an organisation and sometimes their trading partners and they are protected using authentication techniques such as _____.

There are two types of network; a LAN and a _____. LANs are confined to a _____ area and use communication links that are usually owned by the organisation. WANs cover wide areas, often over different countries and use communication equipment such as satellites which are _____ owned by the organisation.

LANs are often _____ in which case they are called WLANs.

There are many security issues with networks including _____ interception, _____ attack and _____ accessing information illegally. To prevent unauthorised access a _____ is used to block outgoing or incoming data if it is suspicious.

Access to computers can be controlled using _____ and passwords. Other authentication techniques involve _____ such as iris scanning, _____ scanning and fingerprint recognition.

Changing passwords _____ means that if someone has managed to find out your password, they can use it only for a short while.

Sensitive data such as credit card numbers are _____ when sent using the internet. Even if the data is intercepted by _____ it cannot be understood.

In many countries the misuse of _____ data is made illegal under a Data _____ act.

Fax communication can be made using a _____ fax which is the traditional method that uses a scanner that scans the page and the data is converted to a series of _____ that are sent along a telephone line. A physical fax converts the sounds back to an image at the other end and prints out the fax.

A more up-to-date method is electronic/internet faxing where the fax is sent and received using the internet. The faxes can be read on the _____ and printed out only if necessary.

10 MINUTE TEST

1 List **four** items from the following which are network devices.

Router   Memory stick   Laser printer
Touch screen   Magnetic tape drive
RFID reader   Bluetooth   Hub
Bridge   3D printer   CRT monitor
Switch

2 Tick true or false next to each statement.

	true	false
A firewall can be used to secure the data in a computer connected to the internet.		
An advantage of video-conferencing is the initial cost of the hardware.		
A web browser is needed to view web pages.		
A WLAN uses fibre optic cables for communication.		
Bluetooth has a greater range compared to WiFi.		

3 Tick true or false next to each statement.

	true	false
Fingerprint recognition can be used as an authentication technique.		
An advantage of networked computers is that fewer printers are needed.		
It is impossible to use a wireless connection to send data from a computer to a printer.		
There is a greater risk from hackers when a computer or network is connected to the internet.		
Viruses do not attack networked computers.		

4 Devices can be linked together so that they are able to share data wirelessly by either WiFi or by using Bluetooth.
  A Explain **one** difference between WiFi and Bluetooth.
  B Describe **one** suitable application for WiFi and **one** suitable application for Bluetooth.

5 A home has four standalone computers and these are going to be networked together to form a small LAN.
  A Give the meaning of the abbreviation LAN.
  B Give the name of the network device that must be present in each computer before they can be networked.
  C It has been decided to set up a WLAN.
    i Describe **one** difference between a wired LAN and a WLAN.
    ii Describe **two** advantages in using a WLAN rather than a wired LAN.

6 Tick true or false next to each of these statements.

	true	false
A bridge always has more than two ports.		
A hub does not manage any of the data traffic through it.		
An intranet uses similar technologies to the internet.		
Switches inspect packets of data so that they are forwarded correctly.		
A firewall is antivirus software.		

7 It is proposed to network six standalone computers.
  A Give **three** advantages of networking these computers together.
  B Give **three** disadvantages of networking these computers together.

The effects of using IT

REVISION SUMMARY

→ Many businesses no longer operate fixed hours. Instead they operate 24 hours per day and 7 days a week. This leads to increased part-time employment. Use of IT means fewer people are needed as computers complete many administrative tasks previously performed by people. The use of **robots** in factories for assembling components, paint spraying and packing parcels reduces the numbers of manual jobs available.

→ As **jobs change with the use of IT**, continual training is needed and new jobs are created such as website designers, programmers, etc. Generally the jobs being created are interesting and demand technical skills. The numbers of shop workers have been reduced as more people shop online.

→ **Jobs where there has been increased employment** include network managers, website designers, IT development staff, delivery staff (to deliver online orders) and programmers.

→ As well as the **increase in part-time work**, many employees are able to **work flexible hours**. Some employees are able to job share or work **compressed hours** (i.e. more hours per day over fewer days).

→ **Microprocessor-controlled devices** now perform many tasks in the home such as washing clothes, controlling heating and alarm systems, cooking food, etc.

Microprocessor-controlled devices such as washing machines increase leisure time; smartphones, tablets and laptop computers increase productivity when travelling.

The use of microprocessors means people do not need to leave the home. Online shopping and banking, the use of downloads for films, books and music, the ability to research things from home mean a lot of trips away from home are no longer needed.

→ There are **health problems** which may develop with the use of computers and these include **back and neck ache**, **repetitive strain injury (RSI)**, **eye strain** and **headaches**. To reduce back and neck ache you can use an adjustable chair and foot support and should sit up straight in the chair. You should ensure that the screen/monitor is positioned correctly.

SYLLABUS

This section will:

- Detail the effects of IT on employment.
- Detail the effects of IT on working patterns within organisations.
- Detail the use of microprocessor-controlled devices in the home.
- Detail the potential health problems related to the prolonged use of IT equipment.

5.1 Effects of IT on employment

The use of IT has increased the number of jobs in some areas but decreased the number of jobs in others and these are summarised in the table on page 48.

Jobs where there have been increased or decreased employment	
Increased	**Decreased**
Website designers	Payroll workers
Computer programmers	Typing pool workers
Delivery drivers delivering online orders	Filing clerks
Computer repair/troubleshooting staff	Factory workers on production lines

5.2 Effects of IT on working patterns within organisations

Working patterns have changed with the introduction of IT in the following ways:

- More part-time working – more organisations operate outside normal office hours so additional staff are needed; many of these can work part-time which suits some people with family commitments.
- Flexible hours – organisations need flexibility so that workers can work when they are needed.
- Job sharing – here you might have several part-time members of staff replacing one full-time member of staff.
- Compressed hours – this allows employees to work longer hours per day but over fewer days.

5.3 Microprocessor-controlled devices in the home

Microprocessor-controlled devices in the home include computers/smartphones, washing machines, children's toys, heating/air conditioning systems, alarm systems, intelligent ovens, microwaves and fridges.

The effects of microprocessor-controlled devices on leisure time

Computers/smartphones – employees can feel that they are at work with little time for family life. Also, playing games/watching movies, etc., can lead to lack of exercise and cause health problems such as obesity.

Washing machines and other devices – free up leisure time but can encourage people to be lazy.

Robot vacuum cleaners/mops – reduced manual work means less exercise unless you use the time freed up to go to the gym.

Use of the internet (e.g. online shopping/banking and social networking sites) can lead to social isolation.

The effect of microprocessors on the need to leave the house

Here are some of the things you can do using microprocessor-controlled devices without leaving your home:

- Online shopping/banking
- Downloads
- Research
- Entertainment
- Working from home.

5.4 Potential health problems related to the prolonged use of IT equipment

A number of health problems are associated with the use of computers and these are summarised here:

Back and neck ache – a painful condition which prevents you sleeping properly and exercising.

How it is caused	How to help prevent it
Not sitting up straight in your chair (i.e. incorrect posture).	Use an adjustable chair (NB in workplaces in some countries this is a legal requirement but you need to ensure that the chair you use at home is adjustable).
Using a laptop on your knee for long periods.	Always check the adjustment of the chair to make sure it is suitable for your height.
Working in cramped conditions.	Use a foot support, called a footrest, if necessary.
	Sit up straight on the chair with your feet flat on the floor or use a footrest.
	Make sure the screen is adjusted so you are looking directly across and slightly down – never to the side or up.

Repetitive strain injury (RSI) – a painful condition causing swelling of the wrist or finger joints.

How it is caused	How to help prevent it
Typing at high speed for long periods without a break.	Take regular breaks.
Using a mouse for long periods.	Use an ergonomic keyboard/mouse. Keep your wrists straight when keying in.
Not adopting correct posture for use of mouse and keyboard.	Learn how to type properly – two finger typing has been found to be much worse for RSI.
Not having properly arranged equipment (e.g. keyboard, mouse, screen, etc.).	Use a document holder.
	Use a wrist rest.
	Position the mouse so that it can be used to keep the wrist straight.

Eye strain/headaches – causes blurred vision and/or headaches.

How it is caused	How to help prevent it
Using the screen for long periods without a break.	Take regular breaks (e.g. every hour).
Working without the best lighting conditions.	Keep the screen clean, so it is easy to see characters on the screen.
Glare on the screen/screen flicker.	Use appropriate lighting (fluorescent tubes with diffusers).
Dirt on the screen.	Use blinds to avoid glare.
	Give your eyes a rest by focusing on distant objects.
	Have regular eye-tests.

Exam preparation

1 Describe **three** fields of employment where there has been an increase in employment due to the introduction of IT.

Exam-style question

1 A i Explain what is meant by the abbreviation RSI.
ii Describe how using a computer can cause RSI.
iii Describe **two** steps that can be taken to minimise the likelihood of developing RSI.
B Other than RSI, describe **two** other health problems that may develop when using computers.

Important things to remember

Fill in the missing key words

IT has changed employment in a number of ways. For example, people need to be more _____ in the hours they work and few will end up doing the _____ job for the whole of their lives. New IT developments mean that constant _____ will be needed to use the new technology. There will be fewer jobs in _____ as more automation is used for assembling products, welding, paint spraying, packing, etc. More people will work from _____ using IT equipment such as video-conferencing for meetings.

There will be reduced employment in areas where manual repetitive tasks are now carried out by _____. There will be fewer workers in _____ as more of us shop online. Job designing and producing CDs/DVDs for films and music will disappear as more of us _____ these.

IT will change working patterns in organisations. There will be _____ availability of part-time work, the opportunity to work _____ hours, the opportunity to job _____ and the opportunity to work compressed _____.

Microprocessor-controlled devices used in the home include computers, children's _____, heating systems, alarm systems and intelligent ovens, microwaves and fridges.

Many of these devices save time and mean that people have more _____ time. Keeping in touch with family is made easier with mobile phones, email and social _____ sites. Cheap international calls over the internet can be made using a service called _____. Many devices such as robot vacuum cleaners, washing machines, etc., perform some of the _____ jobs in the home but this can make you lazy and unhealthy through lack of exercise.

You also do not need to leave your home as _____ as many tasks such as shopping, banking, paying bills, research, entertainment, etc., can be completed using the internet.

Staying at home too much has its problems such as lack of _____ and lack of social interaction with others.

The use of computers can lead to health problems and the main ones are back and neck ache, repetitive _____ injury, eye _____ and headaches. RSI is caused by using a _____ or mouse for long periods without a break. Not sitting upright in your chair can give _____ and neck ache. A dirty screen or screen flicker can give _____.

Back or neck _____ can be caused by incorrect _____. Looking at the screen all day can give you _____. To prevent back or neck ache you should use an adjustable _____ which can be adjusted to the correct height.

(10) *MINUTE TEST*

1 List **four** statements from the following that are drawbacks of using microprocessor-controlled devices in the home.

Can lead to laziness

More family time

Can lead to unhealthy eating

Greater social interaction

Do not need to leave home to get fit

Manual household skills are lost

Can lead to lack of fitness

2 There are health issues associated with the use of computers.
Tick **three** methods which could be used to avoid these issues.

Sit up straight at all times in your chair.	
Make sure there are no trailing wires which could present a tripping hazard.	
Take regular breaks when working at your computer.	
Always use a chair where the height can be adjusted.	
Make sure that waste paper bins are emptied regularly.	

3 Tick true or false next to each of these statements about microprocessor-controlled devices in the home.

	true	false
Washing machines, microwaves, alarms, air-conditioning and computers all make use of microprocessors.		
You do not need to be in the house when clothes are being washed.		
There is less time for social interactions.		
You have to be in the house when food is cooking.		
You can get robots that vacuum and mop your floors automatically.		

4 Repetitive strain injury (RSI) can be caused by the use of a keyboard and mouse for long periods.

Describe **three** steps a computer user can take to minimise the likelihood of suffering from this painful medical condition.

5 A modern home contains many labour-saving microprocessor-controlled devices. Describe the effects that these devices have on people's lifestyles.

6 Microprocessor-controlled devices in the workplace have led to some areas where there has been increased employment and other areas where there has been decreased employment.

A Describe **two** areas of work where there has been increased employment through the use of microprocessor-controlled devices.

B Describe **two** areas of work where there has been decreased employment through the use of microprocessor-controlled devices.

6 ICT applications

REVISION SUMMARY

→ **Communication applications** include using different methods such as newsletters, websites, multimedia presentations, flyers, posters, newsletters, music scores, animations, phones and mobile phones, text messages (SMS), VoIP, letterheads and business cards. All these rely on ICT for their production and use.

→ **Data handling applications** include conducting surveys and processing their results, storing club and society records, producing address lists for mail merges, etc.

→ **Monitoring** involves taking regular readings using sensors over a period of time. Readings can be stored and then presented graphically, used to set off alerts as in an intensive care unit or used to control an automatic device such as a washing machine.

→ **Sensors** usually measure **analogue** quantities such as temperature, pressure, light, humidity, etc., that are continuously variable. As computers process only digital quantities, the analogue values need to be turned into digital values using an **analogue to digital converter**.

→ **Control applications** use the measurements from sensors to decide whether output devices should be turned on or off. Simple control applications include security light systems, burglar alarms and automatic cookers.

→ **Modelling** means producing a series of mathematical equations which are then used to mimic a real situation. Simple models can be produced using spreadsheet software and the figures in the spreadsheet can be altered to see the effect in a series of 'what if...' scenarios.

→ **Robots** used in production lines in factories assemble components, paint panels and pack items in boxes. They have the advantages that they can work continuously, don't need paying, are more accurate than humans and can be re-programmed to perform different tasks.

→ **School management systems** manage the day-to-day administration tasks in a school such as **registration**, keeping **student records**, organising **timetables** and teacher **cover**, organising **examinations**, etc. **Direct data entry** is used wherever possible to reduce the amount of data needing to be typed in and this involves the use of optical mark recognition, smart cards, swipe/magnetic stripe cards and biometric methods.

→ **Online booking** systems use the internet to book tickets. They operate in real time so that seats cannot be double-booked. The advantages of online booking include booking from your home (usually saving money), reading reviews and printing tickets for yourself.

SYLLABUS
This section will:

- Detail communication, data handling, measurement, microprocessors in control and modelling applications.
- Detail the applications in manufacturing industries, school management systems, booking systems and banking applications.
- Detail computers in medicine, computers in libraries, expert systems and computers in the retail industry.
- Detail recognition systems, monitoring and tracking systems and satellite systems.

→ **Banking applications** include the use of automatic teller machines (**ATM**s), online banking where banking is conducted using the internet and phone banking. Money can be transferred between accounts using a system called electronic funds transfer (**EFT**) and it is this system that shops use when taking payments using cards.

→ Computers are used in **medicine** for keeping patient medical records, patient identification using wristbands containing **barcodes**, hospital **intranets**, patient **monitoring**, **expert systems** to aid illness diagnosis and **pharmacy records**. **3D printing** is used in medicine for the printing of prosthetics such as false teeth, artificial limbs, hearing aids, etc.

→ Computers are used in **libraries** where either barcodes or RFID tags are used to input information about members and books into the reserving books, loans, returns and other systems.

→ **Expert systems** use algorithms and programming to mimic the knowledge and decision making of an expert in that field and consist of four components: **knowledge base**, **rules base**, **inference engine** and **user interface**. Expert systems are used, for example, in diagnosing illnesses, mineral/oil prospecting and car engine fault diagnosis.

→ Computers are used in the **retail industry** for scanning goods, issuing itemised receipts and dealing with stock control. Most shops use **EFTPOS** systems where as well as the facilities mentioned, there is also the facility to take card payments so that payments can be made straight to the store's account. These card systems make use of magnetic stripe card readers or the more modern chip and PIN readers. Internet shopping is also popular as there are a wide range of goods available and you can shop at any time of the day.

→ **Recognitions systems** are ICT systems that can automatically identify an object or a person. **RFID** is used in passport control in conjunction with face recognition software to check that your face matches the photograph encoded on the RFID chip. RFID is also used with credit/debit cards in stores for small value payments which saves having to carry cash.

→ **Automatic number plate recognition (ANPR)** systems making use of a camera, and optical character recognition (**OCR**) software to check whether or not to allow a car entry into a car park. It can be also used for traffic enforcement where the number plates are used to identify the vehicle breaking the law.

→ **Public monitoring/tracking** takes place when you use the internet or a mobile phone. In the case of the internet, cookies are used to give the owner of the website information about your browsing activity. Your ISP also monitors your internet use. At work employees are monitored. For example, staff working at checkouts have the number of items put through the till monitored, and drivers have their routes monitored using GPS, and most organisations monitor email and phone use.

→ **Key logging software/spyware** can be put on computers without the owner's knowledge and its purpose is to record passwords and banking details in order to commit fraud.

→ There are two main **satellite systems**: **global positioning systems** (GPS) and **geographic information systems** (GIS). GPS is used to find the precise coordinates of the receiver in terms of latitude, longitude, height above sea level and when used with a map it becomes a satellite navigation system. GIS is a system that is used to capture, manage, analyse and display geographically referenced information.

6.1 Communication applications

There are many ways of communicating using ICT, including: multimedia presentations, websites, flyers, posters, newsletters, music/music scores and animated cartoons.

Other communication applications include mobile phones (for phone calls), SMS (for texting) and VoIP (Voice over Internet Protocol) which is a way of making cheap international phone calls using the internet.

Some documents prepared using ICT are for publicity and to present a consistent corporate image. Such documents include business cards (i.e. small cards containing contact details), letterheads (pre-printed with logo and contact details), flyers and brochures.

6.2 Data handling applications

Many computers are used for data handling applications and these include:

Surveys – preparing questionnaires and then using ICT to read the responses (usually using OMR) and analyse the results (usually using spreadsheet software).

Address lists – contact details are kept so people can be contacted using letters, emails, SMS, phone, etc. It is important that these details can be imported into different software packages.

Clubs and society records – members' details can be kept using database software and these details can be merged with letters to perform mail merges where similar letters are sent to the members.

School reports – school management software has a module to produce school reports and also to store previous reports in case they are needed to provide references in the future.

6.3 Measurement applications

In measurement applications sensors are used to measure physical quantities such as temperature, pressure, light intensity, etc.

Sensors – are input devices which take measurements and input their values into the computer.

Here are the main sensors you should know about:

- Temperature – used for measurements during experiments and for controlling heating/cooling systems.
- Light – measures the intensity of light and used to turn lights on and off automatically.
- Sound – measures the loudness of sounds and used in noise disputes.
- Pressure – used to measure the depth of liquid in a container and also measure the pressure on a pad when a person stands on it.
- Humidity – measures moisture in soil or air in greenhouses or museums/ art galleries.
- Passive infra-red (PIR) – used to detect movement and used in burglar alarms and to turn lights on and off automatically.

Analogue to digital conversion – most physical quantities are analogue (i.e. they don't jump from one value to the next but instead have lots on in-between values) so in order to change the values to digital values, that a computer can understand, an analogue-to-digital converter is needed.

Monitoring – readings from sensors are taken automatically and used immediately for setting off alerts, stored for later processing to produce graphs or for auto control where they are used to turn devices on/off.

Monitoring using ICT	
Advantages	**Disadvantages**
Sensors can be located in inhospitable places (e.g. the North Pole).	Need training to use the equipment.
Readings always taken at exactly the right time.	Equipment is expensive to purchase.
Readings can be taken more frequently than by a human.	Replacing or servicing equipment at remote locations can be inconvenient and costly.
Do not need to pay someone to take the readings.	
No human error when taking readings (i.e. greater accuracy).	
The system does not forget to take a reading.	
Readings go automatically into the computer for reports/alerts.	

6.4 Microprocessors in control applications

Data from the sensors can be input into the microprocessor which then determines whether to turn output devices on or off by comparing the value of the data with a pre-set value. Here are the steps taken:

- A sensor measures the physical quantity (temperature, light, etc.) and inputs the reading into the microprocessor.
- The processor compares the input value with the pre-set value.
- The microprocessor then sends signals to an output device to turn it on or off.
- The process above is continuous.

Control systems	
Advantages	**Disadvantages**
Can operate continuously, 24 hours per day and 7 days per week.	Initial cost of equipment is high.
Less expensive to run as you don't have to pay wages.	Equipment can go wrong leading to poor conditions in the case of greenhouses, offices, etc.
Can easily change the way the device works by re-programming it.	Fewer people needed so leads to unemployment.
More accurate than humans.	
Can react quickly to changes in conditions.	

6.5 Modelling applications

Modelling means producing a series of mathematical equations to mimic a real situation. For example, the money coming into and going out of a business (called cash flow) can be modelled using spreadsheet software.

Examples of computer models include financial models, computer games, traffic flow at junctions, climate change, design of new buildings, etc.

Computer models	
Advantages	**Disadvantages**
Cost – cheaper to produce a computer model (e.g. crash testing a car).	The simulation/model may not accurately reflect reality.
Safer – can model flying an aircraft in extreme conditions.	Mistakes in the rules and variables mean that the model will not produce meaningful results.
It can save time – can create models of global warming.	Some situations are so complex and different people may not agree about the rules used.
Possible to experience more situations (e.g. pilots can experience engine failure).	

6.6 Applications in manufacturing industries

Robots are used in many factories for the assembly of products such as cars, washing machines, computers, etc., and they are also used for the packing of goods.

You can learn about some advantages and disadvantages of using robots rather than humans for these tasks on page 12.

6.7 School management systems

School management systems help in all aspects of running a school such as:

Capturing and processing school attendance details – in many schools OMR is used where a teacher will shade in boxes and the forms are read automatically for input into the computer for processing. This method of direct data entry avoids the use of the keyboard, which is time consuming and less accurate.

In some schools, smart cards containing a computer chip are used for recording attendance and also for payment for meals, gaining access to the school site, networks, photocopiers, etc., as well as for recording the borrowing and returning of library books.

Swipe cards, containing a magnetic stripe can also be used for recording attendance and this can be in a similar way to the smart cards. However, less data can be stored on a magnetic stripe card.

Biometric methods are the ideal way of recording attendance as there is nothing to forget such as a card, the student has to be there to record their attendance and it can be performed in real time. These systems are expensive and there are some privacy issues, particularly with fingerprinting.

School timetabling systems – these systems are able to consider students, teachers, rooms and periods to produce accurate timetables where it is easy to make changes and it can deal with cover for teachers who are absent or rooms that cannot be used.

Organisation of examinations – the examination system ensures students are entered for the correct exams, prints out their exam timetables, identifies suitable rooms and staff to invigilate the exam and finally collects the results and incorporates them into the student records.

School management systems	
Advantages	**Disadvantages**
Reduced workload for teachers means they can focus more on teaching.	The software is expensive to buy.
Parents are provided with up-to-date information at all times.	Lots of personal data is held so there must be no unauthorised access.
The information provided can help decision making by managers (e.g. whether to employ an extra teacher).	Software is complex so the staff will need training to use it.
The information can help tackle truancy.	

6.8 Booking systems

Booking systems are used to book holidays, travel tickets, seats at concerts, etc. Booking systems use online processing – as soon as the transaction is started the seat/holiday, etc., is saved for the user; this prevents double booking.

Online booking	
Advantages	**Disadvantages**
You can book from anywhere at any time.	You have to enter credit/debit card details and these may not be kept safe.
There is more time to look for holidays, flights, etc., than when at a travel agents.	People could hack into the site and know you were away and burgle your house.

Online booking (continued)	
Advantages	**Disadvantages**
You can make savings for flights/holidays when you book direct as there is no travel agent's commission to pay.	Unlike at a booking agent, there is no personal service.
You can read reports from people who have been on the same holiday, seen the same concert, etc.	You could easily enter the wrong information and book the wrong flights or performance on the wrong day.
There is no need to pick up tickets as you often print them yourself or show them on your smartphone.	

6.9 Banking applications

Banks use ICT in the following ways:

ATMs (automatic teller machines/cashpoints) – allow users to obtain cash, check balances, change a PIN, obtain mini statements and top up mobile phones.

The following processing occurs when using an ATM to obtain cash:

- Card is entered and machine reads magnetic stripe or chip.
- User is asked for and enters PIN.
- Machine compares the typed in PIN to that stored (encrypted) on the card.
- If they match, then the machine contacts the bank's computer.
- If they do not match the user is asked to type the PIN again.
- If the user types in the wrong PIN three times the card is retained and the user is told to contact the bank.
- User is asked which service they require. They choose option withdraw cash.
- Bank checks if the amount requested is available in the user's account.
- Bank checks if the amount is within the user's daily/weekly allowance.
- Customer asked if they want a receipt or other services.
- If no other services needed, card is returned to the user.
- If customer wants a receipt then it is printed.
- Machine produces cash/notes for the user to remove.

Benefits to banks in using ATMs	Benefits to customers in using ATMs
Fewer staff needed as some staff are freed from routine tasks.	Some people prefer the anonymous nature of withdrawing money from a machine.
Staff freed from routine tasks so can concentrate on more profitable work.	24 hours a day service is ideal for people who work irregular hours.
24 hours a day service satisfies customer demands.	Fewer queues than in the bank itself.
Customers cannot withdraw more than they are allowed.	If your card is stolen, the thief cannot use your card unless the PIN is known.

Online banking

Many people now use online/internet banking with which they can view statements, transfer money, make payments, apply for loans, etc., from computers or smartphones. To log into online banking you need a username and password, and also answer some other security questions.

Online banking – the bank	
Advantages	**Disadvantages**
Some branches can be closed, which reduces costs.	Customers may move their account owing to less personal service.
Fewer bank workers needed so lower wage bill.	Easier to sell banking products such as loans face to face.
Bank staff can be less qualified which reduces wage costs.	Need to pay out lots of money for redundancies as some staff lose their jobs.
	Specialist staff needed to set up networks to run online banking.

Online banking – the customer	
Advantages	**Disadvantages**
Do not need to spend time travelling to the bank for some bank services.	Worry about hackers accessing your account and stealing your money.
Can perform banking tasks 24 hours per day.	You cannot withdraw cash using the service.
Can pay bills without the need to travel/pay parking, etc.	Lack of personal service that you get with a branch.
Easier to keep track of your balance so less likely to overspend.	

EFT (Electronic funds transfer) – is a method of transferring money electronically from one bank account to another. When a debit card is used to make a payment, the money is transferred from the bank account of the purchaser to the store/organisation. Wages are also paid into employee bank accounts using EFT.

Electronic funds transfer (EFT)	
Advantages	**Disadvantages**
Money can be transferred using any device with internet access.	There is a danger that hackers could intercept the transfer.
Fast transfer of money that can be instantaneous or take a couple of hours.	The charges for the service can be high especially when the accounts are in different countries.
The transfer is secure as the data is encrypted. Hackers will not be able to understand the data even in the unlikely event of them intercepting it.	A mistake in the entry of one of the very long account numbers could result in the money being transferred to the wrong account.
Funds can be sent to anyone who has a bank account, anywhere in the world.	

Phone banking – usually used by people who are wary of using online banking. Most banks require a number and pass-code to use the service and many of the services are automated, which means you do not talk to a real person. The automated services include checking balances, hearing your latest transactions, transferring money between accounts and paying credit card bills. If you speak to an advisor you can also perform these tasks, plus you can stop cheques, order foreign currency, change your personal details, arrange a loan/overdraft or open a new account.

6.10 Computers in medicine

ICT is used in the following ways in medicine:

Medical databases – hold patient medical details which can be accessed from any computer.

Patient identification using barcodes – bar codes are on wristbands which can be scanned so the medical records for that patient can be accessed.

Hospital intranets – use internet technology internally for hospital staff to access patient records, emails, notices, etc.

Patient monitoring – sensors measure vital signs automatically such as temperature, blood pressure, pulse, central venous pressure, blood sugar and brain activity. Signals from the sensors are analogue and need to be changed to digital signals using an analogue to digital converter before being processed by the computer. Some of the signals are processed to produce graphs which show trends over time. Readings from sensors are taken automatically and are constantly compared with pre-set values to check they are within a safe range, and if not an alarm sounds to alert medical staff. Patient monitoring means readings are accurate and it frees up medical staff to do other tasks.

Expert systems – covered in Section 6.12.

Computerised reporting of test results – results of laboratory tests are added to the patient's records.

Pharmacy records – generates labels for drugs and checks if the patient has any allergic reactions to certain drugs.

Producing medical aids using 3D printing – such as false teeth, teeth implants, artificial limbs, hearing aids, artificial blood vessels, etc. Tissue engineering can be used to produce layers of cells to replace damaged tissue. Medical tools can be designed using computer-aided design (CAD) software and then printed in 3D.

6.11 Computers in libraries

All books and members are given a unique number. When a book is borrowed the book number and member number are recorded along with the date from which the return date is calculated. In some systems these numbers are recorded in a barcode which removes the need to type them in. In the latest systems RFID tags are used in the books so that they can be read from a distance, which removes the need for staff to scan books. In all the systems, a relational database is used to hold the details of books, members and loans. The system can produce details of people who have not returned their books on time so they can be sent text messages, emails or letters. If the library is closed, an RFID reader can read the tags on the books being returned at a book drop where a receipt is issued as proof that the books have been returned. RFID tags free up library staff to do other tasks.

6.12 Expert systems

Expert system – uses algorithms and programming to mimic the knowledge and decision making of an expert in that field so that by answering relevant questions a non-expert can be guided towards better decisions than they might otherwise make.

The four components of an expert system are:

User interface – this uses an interactive screen (which can be a touch screen) to present questions and information to the operator and also receives answers from the operator.

Knowledge base – a huge, organised set of knowledge about a particular subject. It contains facts and also judgemental knowledge, which gives it the ability to make a good guess, like a human expert.

Rules base – made up of a series of IF, AND, THEN statements to closely follow human-like reasoning.

Inference engine – uses the input data along with the rules in the rules base and the knowledge in the knowledge base to arrive at conclusions/decisions/answers which are output via the user interface.

The processes involved in a typical expert system such as a medical expert system for diagnosis are as follows:

1 An interactive screen appears and asks the user questions.
2 Answers are typed in or options are selected using a touch screen.
3 The inference engine matches the data input with the knowledge base, using the rules base until matches are found.
4 The system suggests the probable diagnosis and suggests treatments.

Stages for creating an expert system are:

• Experts are interviewed.
• Data is collected from experts.
• Knowledge base is designed and created.
• Rules base is designed and created.
• Inference engine is designed and created.
• Input and output format/screens are designed and made.
• Expert system is checked by using known results.

Expert systems	
Advantages	**Disadvantages**
Fewer mistakes as human experts may forget things.	Lacks common sense. A human can decide whether a conclusion is sensible or ridiculous.
Less time to train. Human experts need years of training/experience.	Lacks senses as it can only react to what is typed in. It cannot look at body language, etc.
Cheaper to use an expert system compared to paying human experts.	Mistakes in the rules could mean the results are incorrect.
More expertise than a single expert as many human experts may create an expert system.	
Always asks a question a human expert may forget to ask.	

Applications of expert systems include medical expert systems – used to diagnose illnesses of patients using the following steps:

The interactive screen asks questions and the doctor enters the answers using a keyboard or touch screen. Using the answers, the interactive interface asks other questions which are answered. The inference engine compares the data entered with that held in the knowledge base and, using the rules base, matches are found. The system suggests possible illnesses with a probability for each.

Other applications for expert systems include:

- Animal or plant identification – guides the user through the complex task of identification.
- Tax – ensures that the correct tax advice is given to businesses and individuals.
- Prospecting for oil/minerals – uses geological information to determine the most likely place to find oil/minerals.
- Car fault diagnosis – guides mechanics through the complex process of identifying a problem with a car engine.
- Careers – asks the user a series of questions about their qualifications, interests, personality in order to suggest suitable future careers for them.
- Chess games – mimics the actions of a human chess player.

6.13 Computers in the retail industry

Point of sale (POS) terminals – are computerised tills in shops that usually use a barcode reader as the input device and which deal with stock control and produce an itemised receipt.

Electronic funds transfer at point of sale (EFTPOS) – same as a POS terminal except they deal with payments. The payments are transferred from your account to the shop's account automatically.

As well as the above, POS/EFTPOS terminals also deal with:

- Cashback – where a debit card is used to obtain cash.
- Loyalty cards – where you are allocated points each time you shop.
- Accounts – where the money coming into and going out of the shop is accounted for.
- Automatic stock control – this is covered on page 64.

Hardware used with POS/EFTPOS terminals includes:

- Barcode reader/laser scanner – used to input an item number coded in the barcode as a series of light and dark lines.
- Keyboard – used to enter item codes if the barcode is damaged.
- Touch screen – often used in restaurants where there are no goods to scan.
- Swipe card reader – used to swipe the magnetic stripes on loyalty cards or credit/debit cards where there is no chip and PIN reader.
- Chip and PIN reader – used by customers to insert their credit/debit cards containing a chip. The system then asks them to enter their PIN (personal identification number) which is a number only they know. This is compared with the number encrypted and stored on the card. If the numbers match, it proves to the system that the customer is the genuine owner of the card and payment is made.

Stock control using POS/EFTPOS terminals

Stock levels can be updated automatically at a point of sale terminal.
Here are the steps carried out:

- The barcode on the item is read by the barcode reader and the item number is input.
- The stock file is searched record by record until a match with the item number is found.
- The number of items in stock is read from the matching record.
- One is subtracted from the number in stock.
- The number in stock is now compared with the re-order number.
- If the number in stock is equal to the re-order number then more goods are automatically ordered from the supplier.
- The new value for the number of that item in stock is written back to the stock file.

Internet shopping – the customer	
Advantages	**Disadvantages**
Goods/services often cheaper because costs lower (i.e. company does not have to pay high rent for town centre shops, reduced number of staff so wage bills are lower).	Shoppers may be worried about entering their card details.
Can buy goods/services at any time of day or night or when shops are closed.	Hard to assess the quality of goods first before ordering.
Goods can be delivered straight to your door.	Sometimes cost of postage and packing is added.
You can buy goods from anywhere in the world.	Harder to return goods when they are faulty or the wrong size.
Wider range of goods to choose from.	Problems with bogus sites where you can pay for goods that never arrive.
No travelling costs to go shopping.	Lack of the personal service you get in a traditional shop.
	Loss of the social pleasure of going shopping.

Internet shopping – the store	
Advantages	**Disadvantages**
No expensively fitted out high street stores to pay for.	Unemployment – staff in traditional shops lose their jobs so redundancy payments are made.
Can sell goods when shops are closed.	Specialist ICT knowledge is needed to set up the site.
Cheaper to keep in touch with customers as they can be emailed.	Business lost abroad if their goods are cheaper.
Can site their warehouse(s) anywhere where rental is cheap.	Networks can fail and this means customers cannot access the store.
Can sell goods to anyone in the world.	Not everyone has access to the internet so you will lose some customers.
Do not need to work long hours like in a shop.	Postage/delivery charges can put people off.
Less shoplifting.	Personal data is kept about customers and this could be targeted by hackers.

6.14 Recognition systems

Recognition systems – computer applications that can automatically identify an object or person and process the data without a human operator being present, thus saving time and money.

Recognition systems using magnetic ink character recognition (MICR), optical mark recognition (OMR), optical character recognition (OCR), and radio frequency identification device (RFID) are covered in Chapter 2.

RFID used in passport control – e-passports contain an RFID chip and when the passport is opened and placed on a scanner next to the automatic barrier, the data on the RFID chip is read. The system runs a face-recognition check using a camera and compares this with your photograph encoded on the chip in your passport. The system uses certain facial characteristics to produce a match and then performs some checks to make sure you're eligible to enter the country and if you are, the gate opens automatically.

RFID used for contactless payments – credit/debit cards, key fobs, smartphones can use (RFID) radio frequency identification for making secure payments. The embedded chip and antenna enable consumers to wave their card or fob over a reader at the point of sale to make a payment. The payment system is available only for low value payments where it is designed to replace having to carry cash. You can also make contactless payments using an app on your mobile phone.

6.15 Monitoring and tracking systems

ICT can be used to monitor and track people and vehicles.

Automatic number plate recognition (ANPR) – uses a camera and optical character recognition (OCR) software to input the number into a computer for processing. Applications include:

Traffic enforcement – the system can check whether or not a vehicle is taxed, recognise cars when they are parked illegally and recognise cars speeding or going through red lights so their drivers can be fined or prosecuted.

Car park management – the system reads the registration number and if allowed into the car park, the barrier is raised. Also used when you have pre-paid a car parking space at an airport. Both systems have the advantage that there is no card or ticket to lose/forget.

Electronic toll collection – the system recognises the car and deducts the toll automatically.

Public monitoring/tracking

Internet service provider (ISP) – records details of your internet browsing activity and any emails or other messages sent.

Cookies – pieces of text that websites put on your computer when you visit their site. Records details of the pages you visited and how long you spent on them.

Phone call tracking – for mobile phones the service provider tracks the calls and the exact position from which they were made. There are two levels to call monitoring:

- Simple recording of numbers called/received and time. Mobile and landline companies normally do this anyway for billing purposes. Records can be investigated by appropriate authorities, e.g. police, in the event of an allegation of a crime.
- Actual recording of content of the calls for legal dispute issues. Companies/ organisations may do this to ensure that customers are being dealt with fairly. Companies may also use this if they have a dispute with a member of staff about their use of the phone in work time.

Worker monitoring/tracking

Workers are monitored/tracked in the following ways:

Supermarket workers – have the number of items passing through the tills over a time period monitored.

Internet use is monitored by network managers – they can check sites visited and how long was spent on them during working time. They can check that no inappropriate sites are visited and no illegal activities are performed (e.g. copyright infringement, online bullying, virus distribution, etc.).

Emails can be read – employers can check that no personal emails are sent during office hours. They can check that the emails are in the house style and present the correct image.

Delivery drivers can have their locations monitored – this system uses GPS to check that drivers are driving the shortest route and not speeding.

6.16 Satellite systems

Satellite systems are used to work out the position of a receiver and they are used in the following ways:

GPS (global positioning system) – a satellite-based system using at least four satellites to work out the position (latitude, longitude, and altitude) of the receiver on the Earth. When the position is combined with a map, the system becomes a satellite navigation system with which many new cars are equipped.

Uses for GPS include:

- Satellite navigation systems for cars.
- Marking out plots of land accurately so there are no future disputes over boundaries.
- Used by walkers so they don't get lost.
- Used by aircraft and ships for navigation.
- Used to work out distance travelled by runners.

GIS (geographic information system) – ICT system used to capture, manage, analyse, and display geographically referenced information. Using GIS you can determine distances between two places, see an aerial view of your home or area where you live, find the nearest petrol station or restaurant, etc.

Satellite navigation systems	
Advantages	**Disadvantages**
Can show you the shortest route thus saving fuel.	Inputting details of a destination while driving can be dangerous and lead to accidents.
Can show you the quickest route, thus saving travelling time.	May send your vehicle down a route which is not suitable, e.g. a large lorry getting stuck down a narrow road.
Can show alternative routes if there is a problem with your planned route.	Information may be out-of-date, e.g. a new one-way system in a city isn't recognised.
Can calculate expected journey time to help you arrive in time or phone to inform the person you are meeting if you will be late.	People may follow instructions even when there is an error, e.g. going the wrong way in one-way system, trying to cross a stream or river during a rainy season.
Can provide information on other services nearby, e.g. petrol stations, banks and cafes.	

Media communication systems – systems using satellite signals rather than terrestrial (land-based) signals for communication. Used by media companies (e.g. TV news) when sending stories/video/pictures from remote locations (e.g. in a desert or up a mountain).

Exam preparation

1 Discuss the advantages and disadvantages of using robots rather than humans in car production lines for the manufacturing of cars.

Exam-style question

1 Microprocessor control systems are used in central heating systems to keep a home at a constant temperature.

   A **i** Explain what is meant by a pre-set value with reference to this system.

      ii Describe the processing that is carried out to keep the room at a constant temperature.

   B Give **two** advantages and **two** disadvantages of using microprocessor control systems rather than a human to control the heating of a house.

Important things to remember

Fill in the missing key words

There are many different ways of communicating using ICT. For example, ICT can be used to prepare paper-based documents such as newsletters, flyer and posters. You can also communicate using _____ messaging, phone calls and websites. A technology called _____ allows cheap international phone calls to be made using the _____.

_____ handling applications include the processing of survey lists, address lists, club and society records, school reports and school libraries.

Computers can be used for measurement and these systems use _____ to input the data automatically. Data can be of two types: _____ and digital. Analogue data does not jump from one value to the next and before this can be processed by a computer it needs to be converted to digital data using an _____ to digital converter.

Microprocessors are also used in control where sensors are used to _____ data into the computer. The value of the data is compared with a _____ value to see whether it is lower, the same as, or higher. The processor can then decide which _____ devices to turn on or off.

Computers can be used for the construction of computer _____ which can be used to construct 'what if' scenarios. Computer-controlled _____ are used for assembling components on production lines and have replaced a lot of repetitive _____ jobs.

Most schools use a computer system called a school _____ system which performs many routine tasks such as keeping records of student details, attendance and marks for tests. These systems can also be used for preparing _____, organising examinations and working out cover for absent teachers.

_____ systems are used by travel, theatre and cinema companies.

These booking systems ensure that seats cannot be _____ booked.

Banks use lots of different IT systems. They use a system called _____ for transferring funds electronically between banks. Computers also control _____ which are popularly called cash machines. They are also used to process credit/debit card transactions and bank _____ using direct data entry using magnetic ink characters.

Computers are used in medicine for the keeping of patient records, pharmacy records and _____ of patients in intensive care departments. _____ systems are used by doctors to aid medical diagnoses. These systems consist of four components: an interactive user interface, an _____ engine, a _____ base and a knowledge _____.

Computers are used in libraries to record books and borrowers. Barcodes are used but many libraries now use _____ tags as they can be read from a distance and hold more information.

Most large stores use EFTPOS terminals where the customer makes a debit/credit card payment using a chip and ____ reader. The validity of the card is checked and the money is transferred electronically from the customer's bank account to the store's bank account.

Recognition systems are used for direct data entry in many different applications such as _____ mark recognition for marking multiple choice examination papers, optical _____ recognition for recognising car number plates on entry to a car park and _____ tags in passports to check if a person should be allowed entry at border control.

To obtain the exact position of a point on the Earth's surface _____ is used and when used with a map this system becomes a _____ _____ system which many people have in their cars.

MINUTE TEST

1. List **four** components from the following that are part of an expert system.

   Interactive user interface

   Computer model

   RFID

   Magnetic ink character recognition

   Knowledge base

   Rules base

   Interference engine

   Inference engine

2. There are many ways data can be automatically entered into a computer system.

   Tick **three** methods of entering data automatically.

	✔
Using a camera and OCR software to recognise a car to allow it entry to an airport car park.	
Typing in monthly expenses into a computer model.	
Making a low value payment at a shop using a debit card with an RFID chip.	
Using OMR to input the responses to a survey.	
Keying in the data to create a business card.	

3. Tick true or false next to each of these statements about expert systems.

	true	false
Expert systems can be used for mineral/oil prospecting.		
Expert systems do not need human experts for their development.		
There are five components of an expert system.		
A rules base is part of an expert system.		
The user is not asked any questions as all the answers are known.		

4. Describe **two** medical uses of a 3D printer.

5. Many people now use internet shopping for their weekly grocery shopping.

   Describe **two** advantages and **two** disadvantages of internet shopping.

6. The network manager of an organisation monitors the use of the internet by its employees.

   A Explain, giving a reason, why the organisation monitors internet use by their employees.

   B The company also records phone calls made to their customers. Give **one** reason why the phone calls are recorded.

7 The systems life cycle

REVISION SUMMARY

→ The **systems life cycle** consists of a series of steps that should be taken when developing a new system or improving an old system.

→ There are six stages: **analysis**, **design**, **development and testing**, **implementation**, **documentation** and **evaluation**.

→ **Analysis**, the first stage, looks at the existing system (if there is one) and investigates the requirements of a new system. Analysis involves research using questionnaires, interviews, observations and examination of existing documentation. A system specification is then produced outlining the hardware and software for the new system. The hardware requirements will include the storage, processor, memory, input devices and output devices needed. The software requirements will include the operating system and the applications software needed.

→ **Design**, the second stage, produces the designs for the new system and this includes designing data capture forms, screen layouts, validation routines, report layouts and screen designs.

→ The third stage, **development and testing**, develops the system from the designs and then tests it. Developing the system includes creating the data/file structures, validation routines, input methods, and output formats; after creation, they all need testing.

→ The fourth stage, **implementation**, involves converting from the old system to the new system and there are several ways in which this can be done: *direct changeover* where you stop using the old and start using the new system, *parallel running* where the two systems are run together for a while, *phased implementation* where parts of the system are gradually implemented and *pilot running* where one branch is converted to the new system and then another and so on.

→ The fifth stage is **documentation** which involves the creation of both user and technical documentation.

→ The sixth and final stage is **evaluation** where the system is reviewed in terms of its efficiency, ease of use and the appropriateness of the solution.

SYLLABUS

This section will

- Detail the systems life cycle including the stages: analysis, design, development and testing, implementation, documentation, and evaluation.

7.1 Analysis

Analysis is the first stage of the systems life cycle; this and the other stages are shown in the diagram:

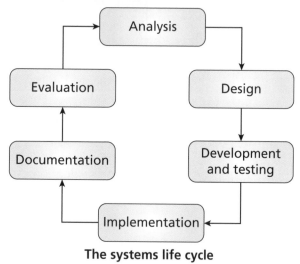

The systems life cycle

Analysis looks at the current system or the requirements of a new system to determine the problem that needs solving, collecting facts about the old or required system to determine the inputs, outputs and processing, to identify problems with the existing system and identify the user and information requirements to solve the problem.

Fact finding about the proposed new system or the existing system can be carried out by:

- Giving questionnaires to users of the current system – ask about the old system and its problems and also what the new system must do.
- Interviewing users of the current system – face-to-face interviews with all staff who use the system are conducted to understand the old system and to understand what the new system must do.
- Observing the users of the current system – can see the old system in use.
- Examining the documents of the current system – looking at any user documentation/guides for the existing system.

Giving questionnaires to current users	
Advantages	**Disadvantages**
More honest answers as they can be completed anonymously.	People often do not return the questionnaires.
You do not have to pre-arrange appointments so easier to collect information.	Questions may be misunderstood giving inaccurate/irrelevant answers.
Much less time-consuming method of getting information from lots of people.	It is hard to design a questionnaire that will collect the information needed.
Questionnaires can be analysed automatically by making use of optical mark recognition (OMR).	There is no-one to ask if a question is unclear.
Less time needed to collect the information than by interviews.	

Using interviews	
Advantages	**Disadvantages**
Questions can be explained if they are not understood.	People may find it intimidating and not give honest answers.
No need to work to a set script so can ask ad-hoc questions in response to answers to other questions.	Very expensive as people need to be taken away from their normal work.
People are likely to take an interview more seriously than a questionnaire.	Person being interviewed cannot remain anonymous.
Questions can be changed to the suit member of staff being interviewed.	The analyst has to conduct them and this makes the technique expensive.
	Very time consuming, especially if lots of people need to be interviewed.

Using observations	
Advantages	**Disadvantages**
Can immediately see the processes involved in the system.	Person being observed may work in a different way from normal.
There is someone to ask about the old and new systems.	Person being observed may feel as though they are being spied on.
It is possible to gain a more accurate view of the existing system.	
It is fairly inexpensive as you are not taking the person being observed away from their work.	

Examining existing documentation	
Advantages	**Disadvantages**
Saves time as there may be copies of previous analysis.	It may waste time if the existing documentation is not relevant to the new system.
Can see existing input and output designs.	It is expensive because of the time it takes the analyst to perform.
It is easy to understand the data flows through the system.	It is very time consuming.
Allows the person doing the analysis to determine the size of system needed using the volume of orders, invoices, etc. as a guide.	

System specification – a document which outlines the hardware and software for the new system. The hardware includes the storage requirements (e.g. hard disk, storage in the cloud, etc.), the processor needed, the memory, input and output devices. The software requirements include the operating system to be used along with the applications software (off-the-shelf or specially written).

7.2 Design

Using the information from the analysis, a design is produced which includes the following:

- Data capture forms (these are forms used for the input of data).
- Screen layouts (these are part of the user interface).
- Validation routines to try to ensure data going into the system is reasonable.
- Verification methods to ensure that data entered into the system is copied accurately from the source.
- Report layouts (this is the output from the system that is printed).
- Screen displays for the output (this is the output from the system that is displayed on the screen).
- Data/file structures (for example, if a database needs to be produced then the tables will need to be designed).

Designing validation routines

Validation routine – checks on data to reduce the possibility of data that is not in the expected range or type from being entered.

Validation checks include:

- **Boolean checks** – data is either: True or False, Y or N, Male or Female.
- **Data type check** – to check that data being entered is the same type as the data type specified for the field. This would check to make sure that only numbers are entered into fields specified as numeric, or letters only in a name.
- **Presence checks** – some database fields have to be filled in, while others can be left empty. A presence check would check to make sure that data had been entered into a field.
- **Length checks** – check a certain number of characters has been entered. For example, in one country a driving licence number has a length of 15 characters. Without the correct number of characters, the data would be rejected.
- **Consistency checks** – checks to see if the data in one field is consistent with the data in another field. For example, if gender is M then there should not be Miss in the title field.
- **Range checks** – are performed on numbers. They check that a number being entered is inside a certain range. For example, all the students in a college are aged over 14, so a date of birth being entered which would give an age less than this would not be allowed by the range check.
- **Format checks** – are performed on codes to make sure that they conform to the correct combinations of characters. For example, a code for car parts may consist of three numbers followed by a single letter. This can be specified for a field to restrict entered data to this format, e.g. DD/MM/YY for a date field.
- **Check digits** – are added to important numbers such as bank account numbers, International Standard Book Numbers (ISBNs), etc. Check digits are placed at the end of the block of digits and are used to check that the digits have been entered correctly into the computer.

When the large number is entered, the computer performs a calculation using all the digits to work out this the check digit. If the calculation reveals that the check digit is the same as that calculated by the other digits, it means that the whole number has been entered correctly.

Deciding verification methods to ensure that data entered into the system is copied accurately from the source

Two methods are used:

Visual checking – comparing what is on a form/document/card with what is typed in to check that both match. This is what you would do after you have typed in details to make an online order when you enter credit/debit card details.

Double entry of data – data is entered twice; only if it matches is it accepted for processing. When you create a new password you usually have to enter it twice to check you have not made a mistake.

7.3 Development and testing

This stage involves creating the new system based on the designs, and then testing it. The following tasks are completed in this stage:

- **Creating the data/file structure and testing it** – involves creating the database tables and entering the field names, the type of each field, the length of the field, etc., and setting up key fields and links between tables. Test data is entered to check the structure.
- **Creating validation routines and testing them** – using the designs, the validation routines are created and checks are thoroughly tested by entering some test data, which will be discussed later.
- **Creating input methods and testing them** – there are many different ways of inputting data into a system. For example, share prices can be input directly from a website and put into a spreadsheet. Many systems will make use of a keyboard to enter data into a form, spreadsheet, etc. As well as creating these methods, they will need to be tested.
- **Creating output formats and testing them** – this involves creating reports, etc., and testing that the information output is complete and that it produces the correct results.

Testing strategies

IT solutions need testing and test data is used with a test plan. Tests are numbered and each test has the data to be used for the test, the reason for the tests and the expected result for the test and a space is left for the actual result and a comment on the result.

Testing using normal, abnormal and extreme data

Testing uses the following three types of data:

- **Normal data** – data that should pass the validation checks and be accepted.
- **Abnormal data** – data that is unacceptable and that should be rejected by the validation check. If data is rejected then an error message should be displayed explaining why it is being rejected.
- **Extreme data** – is data on the borderline of what the system will accept. For example, if a range check specifies that a number from one to five is entered (including one and five) then extreme data used would be the numbers one and five.

Testing using live data – this is a copy of actual data for the existing system. This is used with the new system to check that the results produced are the same as those produced by the old system. Testing takes less time as test data does not have to be created, but the testing is not as thorough as testing using test data.

7.4 Implementation

This stage involves converting from the old to the new system. Here are the four methods of implementation: direct changeover, parallel running, phased implementation and pilot running.

Direct changeover – you stop using the old system one day and start using the new system the next day.

Direct changeover	
Advantages	**Disadvantages**
Fastest method of implementation.	If the new system fails, you might lose all the data.
Benefits are available immediately.	All staff need to be fully trained before the change, which may be hard to time/plan.
Only have to pay one set of workers who are working on the new system.	The old system is removed so there is no system to go back to if things go wrong.

Parallel running – the old system is run alongside the new system for a period until all the people involved with the new system are happy with it. The work is then done entirely using the new system.

Parallel running	
Advantages	**Disadvantages**
If the new system fails then no data will be lost.	You need to pay for workers to enter the data twice; once into the old system and again into the new one.
It allows time for the staff to be trained gradually.	
You have the opportunity to make improvements to the new system before it is fully implemented.	Might be difficult to coordinate, if some workers are on holiday, away on trips, etc.

Phased implementation – a module at a time is implemented throughout the organisation then another module until full implementation.

Phased implementation	
Advantages	**Disadvantages**
Only need to pay for the work to be done once.	If there is a problem, then some data may be lost.
Training can be gradual as staff are trained only one module at a time.	It is suitable only for systems consisting of separate modules.
If the new system fails then the company can still use most of the old system.	It can take a long time before the whole system is implemented.
IT staff can deal with problems caused by a module before moving on to new modules.	There is a cost in evaluating each module before implementing the next.

Pilot running – this method is ideal for large organisations that have lots of locations or branches where the new system can be used by one branch and then transferred to other branches over time.

Pilot running	
Advantages	**Disadvantages**
If the new system fails then it would only affect a small part of the company.	It can take a long time to implement the system across the whole organisation.
Gives an opportunity to evaluate the whole system before it is implemented across the whole organisation.	It is sometimes hard to have one system working differently from the others.
The implementation is on a much smaller and more manageable scale.	

7.5 Documentation

When a new system is implemented, two sets of documentation are produced: user documentation and technical documentation.

User documentation – helps the user learn the new system and deal with any problems. User documentation consists of:

- purpose of the system
- limitations of the system
- hardware requirements
- software requirements
- how to log in/out
- how to run the software
- how to enter data
- how to perform searches
- how to sort data
- how to save
- details of sample runs
- tutorials to help learn the software

- dealing with error messages
- troubleshooting
- frequently ask questions (FAQ).

Technical documentation – is used by the staff who maintain the system and staff who may further develop the system in the future. Technical documentation consists of:

- purpose of the system
- limitations of the system
- hardware requirements
- software requirements
- copies of all the diagrams used to represent the system (program flowcharts, system flowcharts, network diagrams, etc.)
- program listings/program coding
- lists of variables used
- details of known bugs
- sample runs (with test data and results)
- file structures (e.g. structure of database tables, etc.)
- validation routines used
- user interface designs
- test plans
- meaning of error messages.

7.6 Evaluation

Once the new system is working it can be evaluated by looking at the efficiency, the ease of use and the appropriateness of the solution.

There are a number of evaluation strategies that can be used to evaluate the solution and these include:

- Comparing the solution with the original task requirements – to check that the requirements have been met.
- Identifying any limitations and necessary improvements to the system – so that the system works without any problems.
- Ask users about their opinion of the new system – to determine how easy the system is to use.
- Evaluate user response to using the new system – to take into account user needs (e.g. if better user documentation/more user training is needed).

Exam preparation

1 When a new computer system is produced, two types of documentation are produced: user documentation and technical documentation.

Here are some items of documentation. By placing a tick in the relevant column indicate whether the item of documentation belongs to user documentation, technical documentation or both.

Documentation	User	Technical	Both
Hardware and software requirements.			
How to use the system.			
Limitations of the system.			
Frequently asked questions.			
Troubleshooting guide.			
Test plans.			
Purpose of the system.			
Program listings/program code.			
User interface designs.			

Exam-style questions

1 A new library system is being implemented in a school. The person who developed the system is choosing between two methods of implementation which are:

Parallel running

Direct changeover.

A Describe **two** advantages and **two** disadvantages in using parallel running as the method of implementation.

B Describe **two** advantages and **two** disadvantages in using direct changeover as the method of implementation.

2 Explain, by giving examples, the difference between validation and verification.

Important things to remember

Fill in the missing key words

The _____ is the series of stages that have to be completed in order to create a new or modified computer system. It consists of _____ stages, the first of which is the _____ of the existing or proposed new system. At the end of this stage a document called the _____ _____ is produced which outlines the hardware and _____ for the new system.

After the analysis, the _____ stage produces the designs for the system. Data _____ forms are designed for the input of data, screen _____ are produced for the user interface, _____ routines are designed to prevent invalid data from being entered and details of output designs are produced.

_____ _____ _____ is the next stage and in this stage the system is produced and tested. A _____ _____ is produced that will include all the data that is used to test the parts of the system. Normal, _____ and extreme data are used to test the system.

The _____ stage is the stage where the users change from one system to another. There are four methods of implementation: direct changeover, _____ running, _____ implementation and pilot running.

The next stage is the _____ stage where both user and technical documentation are produced.

The sixth and last stage is the _____ stage, where the efficiency of the solution, the ease of use and the appropriateness of the solution are looked at.

1 Tick true or false next to each of these statements.

	true	false
Analysis looks at the current system or the requirements of a task.		
The development and testing stage comes after the implementation stage.		
Using questionnaires is a method of implementation.		
A system specification is produced during the analysis stage.		
Validation routines are designed in the development and testing stage.		

2 Tick true or false next to each of these statements.

	true	false
Validation checks will always prevent wrong data from being entered.		
A presence check can be used with a field such as gender which must always be entered.		
Range checks are performed on numbers.		
Double entry of data is a method of validation.		
Visual checking is a method of verification.		

3 After a new system has been designed it must be implemented. There are a variety of ways in which a system can be implemented. Give **one** advantage of each of the following methods of implementation.
  A Parallel running
  B Direct changeover
  C Phased implementation

4 A new system is being tested. A field with a range check is being tested. The range check allows a whole number between 1 and 50 to be entered. Each of the following items of data is being used to test the range check. Tick whether each of these items of data is an example of normal data, abnormal data or extreme data.

	Normal data	Abnormal data	Extreme data
0			
1			
Twenty five			
15.5			
34			
50			

5 In a store which sells children's toys, none of the toys costs more than $40.
  A Give the names of **two** validation checks that could be used with the toy_price field.
  B Identify **three** items of test data which could be used with the toy_price field, giving reasons for your choices.

Safety and security

REVISION SUMMARY

→ **Physical safety** is about ensuring people do not come to any harm while working with computer equipment. Physical safety issues include **overheating** due to the heat generated by computers, fire caused by **overloaded power sockets**, **tripping over cables**, **electrocution** caused by drink spillage and injuries caused by heavy equipment falling.

→ **e-safety** is about using the internet in a safe and responsible way. e-safety involves making sure you do not meet anyone from online on your own, never revealing personal information online, using only recommended websites, not opening emails or attachments unless you know who they are from and so on.

→ When playing online computer games you should not reveal personal information or install software illegally.

→ e-safety also covers ensuring the **security of data** on your computer and making it difficult for hackers to gain access to personal data such as bank/card details or passwords.

→ **Authentication techniques** are used to check that the person accessing the internet/network services is genuine. Authentication techniques include the use of usernames and passwords, digital certificates and biometric methods.

→ **Usernames** identify the user to the system, and **passwords** ensure that the person using the username is authentic. Passwords should consist of a combination of upper and lower case letters, numbers and punctuation marks/symbols. You should not write your password down or tell it to anyone who asks, and it should be changed regularly.

→ Some computers/networks use **biometrics** rather than passwords to authenticate users. These include **fingerprinting**, **iris** or **retinal scanning** and **face recognition**. The advantage of biometric methods is that there is nothing to forget, like a password.

→ **Online transfer of data** such as some emails, bank/credit card details need to be kept confidential. Digital certificates provide identifying information that is forgery resistant and allows information to be securely communicated over the internet. **SSL (secure socket layer)** is a standard for encryption of card/bank details.

SYLLABUS
This section will

- Detail the physical safety issues when working with computers and describe simple strategies for preventing these issues and minimising the potential safety risks.
- Detail the e-safety issues when working with computers.

8.1 Physical safety – ensuring you are not harmed when working with computers

The main physical safety issues are summarised in the table on page 83.

Safety hazard	Cause	Prevention
Overheating	Computer circuits produce lots of heat which can cause a fire.	Install air-conditioning. Install smoke-detectors.
Fire	Overloaded power sockets.	Wire computer rooms with plenty of sockets.
Tripping	Trailing cables pose a tripping hazard.	Sink cables into floor or under floor covering. Use wireless technology to reduce number of cables.
Electrocution	Faulty equipment or liquid spills.	Do not tamper with equipment. Keep drinks away from computers.
Heavy equipment falling	Incorrectly balancing equipment.	Position equipment properly.

8.2 e-safety – using the internet in a safe and responsible way

Your personal safety can be compromised if you give personal information to people you do not know. To be safe, never reveal:

- your real name
- your address
- the name of your school
- a picture of you in school uniform.

All of the above can be used to identify you and people could harm you.

In addition you could be subject to abuse or bullying if people find out your phone number or email address.

Precautions to be taken when using the internet

- Never arrange to meet an online 'friend' on your own – always take a responsible adult with you.
- Never reveal personal information such as your name, address, school name, photograph, or any other information from which you can be identified.
- Use only websites that are recommended by teachers or your parents.
- Do not open an email from an unknown person.
- Do not open attachments to emails from people you do not know.
- Only send emails to people you know.
- Do not use your real name when playing games online.
- Use a search engine which has a parental guidance setting which your parents can set so that it filters out any unsuitable content.
- Know how to block and report unwanted users in chat rooms.

Precautions to take when playing online games

Here are some measures you need to take in order to stay safe:

- Do not reveal any personal information such as name, address, email, phone numbers and passwords when playing online games.
- Ensure you have antivirus/antispyware software installed to help protect against viruses/identity theft.
- Download games only from a reputable source. Illegally obtained games are often sources of viruses.

8.3 Security of data

To protect against identity theft, you should take steps to keep your personal data secure.

Hackers and hacking – hacking is the process of accessing a computer system without permission and the person who does it is called a hacker. Hackers sometimes just look at the data; others alter it or use it to commit fraud.

The effects of hacking include:

- stealing credit/debit card details for identity theft/fraud
- stealing important commercial information which is sold to competitors
- stealing passwords to gain access to online services (e.g. ISP for internet access, access to your cloud storage, etc.)
- stealing all your email addresses to use for the sending of spam
- using your computer without your permission for sending spam.

Measures to protect data from hackers include:

Using a firewall – a firewall is hardware, software or both that will look at the data being sent or being received by your computer to either allow it through or block it. It can detect hackers trying to access your computer using the internet and it can block the attempt.

Using authentication techniques – to check that a person accessing a network or communications system is the genuine person. They can also be used to ensure that an email sent by a person is genuinely from them and not somebody pretending to be them.

Authentication techniques include:

Usernames and passwords – a **username** is a unique series of characters that is used to identify a certain user to the network. The username is used to allocate certain network resources to the user such as access to files, disk space for their own files, etc.

A **password** is a string of characters (letters, numbers, and punctuation marks) that the user selects. Only the user will know what the password is and the password is not shown on the screen as it is entered.

Biometrics – uses features of the human body unique to a particular person such as a fingerprint, the pattern on the iris (the coloured area surrounding the pupil) and the pattern of blood vessels on the retina (the back of the eye).

Biometric methods for the authentication of a user have the following advantages and disadvantages:

Biometric methods	
Advantages	**Disadvantages**
There is nothing to forget such as a key fob, card, etc.	Some people worry about the privacy of data stored – especially fingerprint details.
You do not have to remember passwords and usernames.	The readers are quite expensive.
It is almost impossible to forge a fingerprint, face, etc.	
It is easy for someone else to access a card, fob, etc., but with a biometric method, the person allowed access has to be present.	

The security of data online

Services such as email, banking, shopping, etc., need to be protected against malicious actions and here are some methods used:

Digital certificate – An electronic passport that allows a person, computer or organisation to exchange information securely using the internet. The digital certificate provides identifying information and is issued by a trusted body.

SSL (Secure Socket Layer) – a standard used to make secure transactions using the internet. SSL allows an encrypted link to be set up between two computers connected using the internet and it protects the communication from being intercepted thus preventing details such as credit card and banking details and other personal information from being stolen and used maliciously. You can tell when SSL is being used on a secure server as the web address begins with 'https' and there is a padlock shown on the page.

Ensuring the security of banking and credit/debit card details and passwords

There are people who will try to trick you into revealing your bank/card/personal details so they can steal your identity and commit fraud. Here are three methods they use:

Phishing – fraudulently trying to get people to reveal usernames, passwords, credit card details, account numbers, etc., by sending emails pretending they are from a bank/credit card company. They usually say that there has been a problem with your account and ask you to update (reveal) information such as passwords, account details, etc. Under no circumstances should you reveal this information. If you do, your identity can be stolen and then details may be used to commit fraud.

Pharming – malicious programming code is stored on a computer and when you try to access a genuine website such as your bank's website you will be taken by the programming code to a fake website which looks genuine. The fake or bogus website is used to obtain passwords or banking details to be used fraudulently.

Smishing – combination of the terms SMS and phishing and it uses text messaging (SMS) rather than emails to send fraudulent messages in an attempt to steal your credit card, banking or other personal details. Some of these messages may say you have won a prize or that your account details need updating, and if you click on the link you will be taken to a fraudulent website where you will be asked to enter your personal details. If you enter your details then it is likely that your details would be used fraudulently.

The security offered by moderated and un-moderated forums

Online forums are places on the internet where people can join discussions on almost any subject and add their comments. There are two types of forum:

Moderated forums – these have a person called a moderator who checks the comments before posting them on the forum. They check that posts are not spam, are not rude or offensive and do not wander off the topic being discussed.

Un-moderated forums – allow people to post whatever they want on the forum, so you may get rude and offensive messages. The forums may be used by people pretending they are something they are not and they may use the forum maliciously. They may use the forum to try to obtain personal details about you.

Spam

Spam is email that is unasked for and is sent automatically to multiple recipients, usually about things you are not interested in. Most spam takes the form of advertisements.

Problems with spam include:

* It can take time looking at the email names of spam before deleting it.
* Spam can sometimes be used to distribute viruses.
* It can clog up your mailbox.
* Spam slows the whole of the internet down for everyone.

Removing spam – spam can be removed using spam filters. These can detect whether or not an email is spam and if it is spam it is removed and put into a spam folder. You can then quickly check if any legitimate email has ended up in the folder and then delete the spam all in one go.

Recognising spam emails and how to avoid being drawn into it

- Look at the email address. If contains strings of alphanumeric characters before the @ symbol, then it is probably spam.
- Look at the email address to see if you are familiar with it or it has the person's name followed by @name of organisation.com. For example, stephendoyle@oup.com
- If there is a link in the body of the message where you have to click on a link to correct something (e.g. keep your continued use of a service) then it is likely to be spam.
- Asking you to do something immediately or quickly indicates spam. This is because the email you will be replying to is changed after a couple of days so the spammers do not get caught.
- Spelling and grammatical errors often indicate spam. Often they originate from different countries so they are not as familiar with spelling and grammar.
- Look for emails that say that they are from your bank, credit card company, internet service provider, etc. If they were genuine, they would never ask for your account or other personal details.
- Genuine emails would address you by your name or have the first or last few digits of your credit card number or account number. If the email addresses you generically (e.g. Dear member, Dear customer, etc.), then it is likely to be spam.

Encryption

Encryption is used to protect data from hackers by scrambling the data as it is transferred using the internet. As the data is scrambled, even if a hacker accesses the data, they will not be able to understand it. When the data is scrambled, an encryption key is used. Only the authorised person being sent the information will have the decryption key that allows them to unscramble the information. Encryption is used when paying by credit/debit card, transferring money between accounts, sending payment details, confidential emails and for storing personal details on laptops or portable media.

Benefits of encryption	Drawbacks of encryption
It allows sensitive personal data to be kept private.	It allows criminals/terrorists to communicate with each other securely.
Data is scrambled so it cannot be understood if it is intercepted by hackers.	It cannot protect the data from being deleted as it is being transferred.
Only the person with the decryption key can decipher/unscramble the data.	

Virus attack/infection

Computer virus – program that replicates (copies) itself automatically and can cause harm by copying files, deleting files, slowing up your computer, spying on your online use or corrupting files. Once a computer or media has a virus copied onto it, it is said to be infected.

To prevent a virus attack you should:

- install antivirus software
- keep the antivirus software up-to-date
- perform regular scans (scans can be scheduled to run automatically on a certain day and time each week)
- not open file attachments to emails unless you know who they are from
- not allow anyone to attach portable drives or memory sticks to your computer unless they are scanned for viruses first
- not download games and other software from a site on the internet unless it is a trusted site.

The dangers of using a credit/debit card online

Here are some ways fraudsters can obtain your credit/debit card details and other personal information:

- The use of key logging/spyware software – software put on your computer without your knowledge to record your keystrokes allows a fraudster to obtain your passwords, credit card details, and personal information. Once they have enough information they can steal your identity and commit fraud.
- The use of bogus sites – sites similar to genuine sites except their purpose is to steal your card and personal information when you make purchases.
- The use of pharming, phishing, and smishing to trick you to reveal card and personal details in response to messages you receive on your computer or mobile phone.
- Hacking into secure sites to obtain the details – if the details are encrypted, they will be of no use to the hacker.

Security of data in the cloud

Storage in the cloud is a way of storing data in one place so that it can be accessed by all your devices as long as you have internet access. Basically you store your files on a file server in a remote place (called the cloud) and you access your files using a user-ID and password.

There are a number of security issues with data stored in the cloud and these include:

- The company providing the storage could go out of business. If this happens then you have to consider what would happen to your data.
- Some of the data could be personal data, in which case it should be encrypted so that if it is hacked into, hackers would not be able to understand and use the data.
- You have to trust that the organisation providing the storage puts in all the security measures to keep your data safe.
- Who owns the data when it is stored in a cloud? When photographs are stored using some cloud storage organisations, you have to give permission that anyone can access and use the photographs you store.

Physical security

Not all security problems come from the internet; you have to protect your computers from access by others directly. Methods of physical security can be used such as:

- Locking doors to rooms containing computers.
- Not leaving your computer logged in when you are away from your desk.
- Ensuring that there are no shoulder surfers looking at your screen when passwords are entered.

Exam preparation

1   **A**   Explain what is meant by a computer virus.
    B   Explain what is meant by hacking.

Exam-style questions

1   **A**   Explain what is meant by the term e-safety when using the internet.
    B   Describe **three** measures to ensure your e-safety when using the internet.

2   Explain what is meant by the following terms:
    A   Spam
    B   Encryption
    C   Digital certificate

Important things to remember

Fill in the missing key words

_____ safety is about ensuring that you do not come to any harm while working with computer equipment. Computers produce lots of heat and can cause an unhealthy working environment which can be solved by installing _____. Using _____ power sockets can lead to _____ and this can be solved by installing plenty of power sockets in computer rooms. Cables present _____ hazards and this safety issue can be solved by sinking or covering cables with carpet. Spilling drinks over computer equipment can cause _____ and to minimise the danger, liquids should not be allowed near computers.

_____ is about using the internet in a safe and responsible way. There is a dangerous side to the internet so you need to keep yourself _____. This means taking precautions such as not agreeing to _____ an online friend on your own, or giving out _____ details, and only using websites suggested by parents or teachers.

_____ is the process of accessing a computer system without permission. Hackers seek to steal and use personal information such as _____ card and banking details to commit fraud.

_____ techniques are used to ensure that the user of a network/internet is genuine. _____ known only to the user, digital certificates and biometric methods are used to authenticate a user.

To ensure the security of messages sent using the internet _____ certificates can be used to ensure that a message sent by someone is definitely from them and not by someone pretending to be them. When goods are paid for on a website, card details are entered using a system called _____ socket _____ which encrypts the details so that if they are intercepted by _____ the details cannot be understood.

People often try to obtain your bank/card details using the following methods:

_____ is where malicious programming code is stored on a computer and when the user tries to access a genuine site, the program directs them to a bogus site which attempts to steal their banking details. _____ uses emails pretending to be from a bank, building society, credit card company, etc., and they usually ask you to confirm your banking details which are then used to commit fraud. _____ uses text messaging (SMS) to send fraudulent messages that try to steal your credit card, banking or other personal details.

An online forum is a discussion on the _____. _____ forums have a person called a moderator who checks the comments before posting them on the forum. _____ forums allow people to post whatever they want on the forum so you can get rude and offensive messages.

_____ is unrequested email that is sent automatically to multiple recipients. It is a nuisance because it takes time to read and _____.

A _____ is a program that replicates (copies) itself automatically and can alter or _____ files. Viruses can be detected and removed using _____ software and to be useful the computer must be _____ regularly and the software _____ regularly.

Many people now store data in the cloud and this means that it is stored on a server somewhere which is regularly _____ up so you need not worry about taking backups yourself.

10 MINUTE TEST

1 Tick true or false next to each of these statements.

	true	false
Phishing uses emails to obtain personal information such as passwords and card details.		
Pharming uses malicious programming code which is loaded onto your computer without your knowledge.		
Smishing is a virus that deletes personal data from your computer.		
Spam is a type of encryption technique used when sending banking details using the internet.		
Encryption scrambles personal data when it is sent using the internet.		

2 Tick true or false next to each of these statements.

	true	false
A virus is a program that copies itself automatically and so can spread to many computers.		
Key logging software is used to help you keep track of your passwords.		

Antivirus software can scan your computer for viruses and then help remove them.		
You should never follow a link and then enter your credit card details.		
Antivirus software is never updated.		

3 Describe each of the following methods that are used by others to try to steal your banking details and your passwords to online services.
   A Phishing
   B Pharming
   C Smishing

4 **A** Explain, by giving a suitable example, the difference between the terms e-safety and physical safety.
   B Describe **two** physical safety issues, saying what causes them and what can be done to prevent them.

5 Describe the difference between a health risk and a physical safety risk.

6 Passwords are used to help prevent unauthorised access to computer systems.
   A Explain, by giving suitable examples, **three** characteristics of a good password.
   B There are other methods that can be used to authenticate the user of a computer system.
   Give the names of **two** other methods of authentication and describe how they are used.

9 Audience

9.1 Audience appreciation

When creating an ICT solution (i.e. publication or product) you must first think about the audience it is aimed at and what their needs might be. As part of this, you can find out:

How much they know already – so that the material is at the right level (beginners, advanced, etc.).

What level of literacy they have – this will determine the sentence length, the use of long words, etc.

How much specialist vocabulary they understand – if they are beginners then all the terms will need to be explained.

Suppose a history website is aimed at children and a different history website is aimed at adults. Here is a table that outlines the differences in their needs:

Website aimed at children	Website aimed at adults
Lots of images.	Images more appropriate for adults.
Uncluttered page design.	More complex page design.
Very easy navigation.	More complex navigation.
Lots of bright colours.	More subtle colours used.
No long words or sentences.	Longer words and sentences.
Uses fun animations such as cartoons.	More subtle cartoons, used sparingly.

9.2 Legal, moral, ethical and cultural appreciation

Legal aspects of copyright

Whenever you produce something original such as some text, a picture, a photograph, a design, a program, some video, etc., you are protected against having it copied or used by others. You may have seen the copyright symbol © being used to draw people's attention to the fact that it is copyrighted.

Copyright legislation

Copyright legislation are laws which make copying illegal without the permission of the copyright owner or paying for the appropriate licence.

Software piracy – the illegal copying of software is called software piracy.

Moral and ethical aspects of software piracy

Here are some of the moral and ethical aspects of software piracy:

- It is against the law and you may be prosecuted, fined or jailed.
- It deprives the creator of payment for their work.
- Companies will not invest in the creation of new software if they are unable to make a profit due to software piracy. This could mean software would not be developed and improved in future.
- Criminals are sometimes involved in software piracy and use money they get from selling cheap unlicensed software to fund other illegal activities such as selling drugs and people trafficking.

Actions that software producers can take to prevent illegal copying

There are a number of actions software producers can take to prevent their software from being copied and these include:

- **Encryption of the execution code** – the execution code enables the software to run. This code is encrypted and a key is needed to unlock the code to enable the software to be used.
- **Use of an activation key** – when you purchase software, after loading it on your computer, you will be asked to activate the software by going onto the software producer's website and then entering a product activation key (a long code).
- **Use of a dongle** – a dongle is a piece of hardware that attaches to a computer using the USB port and allows a secured piece of software to run. The dongle contains an electronic key that unlocks the program on the computer and allows it to run. Making a copy of the dongle is hard.
- **Use of programming code** – the program code can be altered to help block copying.
- **Use of guards** – guards are hardware or software modules that keep a check of the program as it is being run to check that it has not been tampered with in any way.

Social implications

Many ICT developments have social implications. For example, online shopping is cheaper but you can take advantage of the lower prices only if you have a credit/debit card.

Here are some other social implications for ICT developments:

Social exclusion – with no access to ICT, people feel left out.

Job losses – as ICT does many of the tasks previously carried out by people.

Isolation – people without access to ICT cannot access email, SMS, social media, etc.

Policing the internet

Policing the internet is covered in Chapter 4 and here we will just look at the main legal problem of policing the internet.

The internet is global and it may be hard to define which country's laws should be applied to the content – for example, should you consider:

- the country where the surfer is?
- the country where the site owner is registered?
- the country where the server holding the data is?
- the country where the company hosting the site is based?
- the country where the internet service provider is based?

Exam preparation

1 Software piracy is a problem for manufacturers of software.
   A Explain what is meant by software piracy.
   B Explain **two** reasons why software manufacturers are concerned about software piracy.
   C Give **one** reason why you should never buy software that you know is pirated.

Exam-style questions

1 Some people say the internet should be policed.
   A Give **two** reasons why the internet should be policed.
   B Describe why policing the internet would be very difficult.

2 It is morally and ethically wrong to copy copyrighted material illegally. Explain **two** reasons why.

Important things to remember

Fill in the missing key words

When designing and developing an ICT publication or product, you need to consider the intended _____ who could be adults, teenagers, etc. Different audiences have different _____ which must be met.

Illegal copying of computer software is called software _____. Copyright _____ makes it an offence to copy or steal computer software. It also makes it an offence to copy any other _____ work such as text, images, music, designs of user interfaces, etc. Copying software illegally is no different from stealing as it deprives someone of _____. In some cases the selling of illegal software, music and films is used to fund other _____ activities such as selling drugs and people trafficking. You should not download illegally copied software/games as they are often used to distribute _____ which can infect your computer.

One method software producers use to prevent illegal copying of software is by the use of a _____ which can be either hardware or software. Some software producers _____ the execution code of the software so that a key is needed to unlock the code and allow the software to run.

 **MINUTE TEST**

1 Tick true or false next to each of these statements.

	true	false
Copyright laws only cover computer software.		
It is always illegal to copy computer software.		
Copying software illegally is called software piracy.		
Software licences usually allow software to be copied under certain circumstances (e.g. backup copies).		
Copying software onto more than one computer is always illegal.		

2 Tick true or false next to each of these statements concerning methods of preventing copyrighted software from being illegally copied.

	true	false
Encryption of the execution code means that a key is needed to run the software.		
A piece of hardware that attaches to the USB port to allow secured software to run is called a dangle.		
An activation key is sometimes used which is long code that needs to be typed in when on the software manufacturer's website.		
Guards are hardware or software that monitor whether programming code is altered in some way.		

3 A website is being created for young children.

Describe **three** things you would need to consider in the design of this website in order to meet the needs of a young audience.

4 Most countries have copyright laws.

A Explain **two** reasons why copyright laws are needed.

B Describe **three** methods software manufacturers use to prevent their software from being copied illegally.

10 Communications

REVISION SUMMARY

→ **Emails** are electronic messages sent between computers and all web browser software comes with email facilities.

→ **Groups** are lists of people with their email addresses who share a certain characteristic such as relatives, good friends, work colleagues, etc. You can send the same email to a group rather than send lots of individual emails and this saves time.

→ **Constraints that affect the use of email** include obeying the laws that apply, using acceptable language, obeying copyright, obeying local guidelines set by an employer/school, protecting passwords by not putting them in an email, ensuring security and obeying 'netiquette'.

→ **Spam** email is unsolicited email (i.e. not asked for) sent in bulk which clogs up your mailbox/inbox, slows down networks and takes time to delete. **Spam filters** are able to recognise most spam and put it in a folder for deletion.

→ A **web browser** is applications software that provides a graphical user interface to view web pages stored on the internet. A **search engine** is applications software installed on a server that you can access using your web browser, allowing you to search for specific information.

→ There are lots of terms used when talking about the internet, the definitions for which you must remember and these include: **protocol, HTTP, HTTPS, URL, hyperlink, ISP and FTP**. The definitions for all of these are included in the chapter.

→ There are differences between an intranet, the internet and the world wide web (www).

→ An **intranet** is a private network that uses the same technology as the internet, but is accessible only to certain people.

→ The **world wide web** is a means of accessing information contained on the internet and makes use of web browsers to view the information contained on web pages.

→ The **internet** is a huge network of networks and it provides access to web pages, instant messaging, FTP, etc.

→ **Blogs** are online diaries, usually by one author about their life, and the events are arranged in chronological order. Only the person who creates the blog can edit it.

→ **Wikis** are web pages that can be edited by anyone who has a web browser and they usually have many authors and the content is determined by the contributors.

→ **Social networking sites** – help build online communities and allow a user to search for people they have lost contact with. Users can create profiles with their interests, jobs, past achievements, etc.

SYLLABUS

This section will

- Cover the use of communication using email.
- Cover the effective use of the internet.

10.1 Communication with other ICT users using email.

An email is an electronic message sent from one communication device (computer, telephone, mobile phone, or tablet) to another. All web browser software has email facilities.

Timesaving features of email include:

Search – used to find an email using keywords in the title or to search for all the emails from or to a certain email address.

Reply – the recipient is sent both the original email and your reply so they can save time because they know what your email is about and they do not have to enter your email address.

Forward – if you are sent an email that you think others should see, you can forward it to them.

Address book – in the address book are the names and email addresses of all the people to whom you are likely to send email and you just click on a name to select it.

Groups – lists of people and their email addresses. Every time you need to send the members of the group email, you could just send one email to the group, thus saving time.

File attachments – you can attach files to emails. If you can store it as a file, then you can attach it to email, provided the file is not too large.

Constraints that affect the use of email

Constraints affecting the use of email include:

The laws within a country – email is monitored and some email is read in some countries, meaning that you cannot criticise the government or talk about certain topics freely.

Acceptable language – you should always be polite in an email and avoid the use of bad language.

Copyright – copyright laws apply to text in emails. This means that if you pass on a block of text or send a picture to others without the copyright owner's permission, then this would be illegal.

Local guidelines set by an employer – most employers will set out in your contract of employment what you can and cannot do using email and if you do not obey these rules then you would be in breach of your contract and could be dismissed.

The need for security – emails containing personal information should be encrypted to prevent hackers from understanding the information if they manage to hack into the email.

Password protection – email services are protected by passwords and it is up to the user to protect this password and ensure that is not disclosed to anybody.

Netiquette – when using email, you must learn to abide by certain rules such as not typing in all capitals, ensuring file attachments are not too large, not divulging personal information in emails, making emails concise, using plain text and remembering to attach files if there are any.

Spam

Spam – the same email sent in bulk to large numbers of people that didn't ask for it and usually contains advertisements for services that don't interest most people, such as medications and products of an adult nature. People who send spam emails are called spammers.

Why spam needs to be prevented

Spam needs to be prevented because:

- Spam clogs up your inbox.
- Spam takes time to delete.
- Spam can be used to spread computer viruses and malicious software.
- Unnecessary email slows down the internet and other networks.
- Young children could view inappropriate messages or images.

Methods used to help prevent spam

Here are some methods that can reduce the amount of spam you receive:

- Use spam filters – software that is able to recognise what is and isn't spam. Spam emails are put into a separate folder and can then be deleted.
- Avoid publishing your email address on websites, blogs, forums, and suchlike – spammers often use these to collect email addresses.
- Check the privacy policy when signing up for things online – check they won't sell your email address to a spammer.
- Change your password for internet access regularly and use strong passwords – this will keep out hackers who may steal all your email addresses in your address book to sell to spammers.

10.2 Effective use of the internet

The differences between an intranet, the internet, and the world wide web (www)

Intranet – a private network that uses the same technology as the internet for sending messages/data around a network. The main use of an intranet is to share organisational information and share resources. The intranet can be used only by people given permission to use it, and it is protected by passwords. If allowed, users can access the intranet using the internet.

The internet – a huge network of networks. Each computer on the network, provided it has permission, can access the data stored on other computers on the network and also transfer messages between computers. The internet provides services including email facilities, instant messaging and FTP (File Transfer Protocol).

The world wide web (www) – the world wide web is a means of accessing information contained on the internet. It is an information sharing model that is built on top of the internet. The world wide web uses http, which is one of the languages used over the internet, to transmit information and it makes use of web browser software to access documents called web pages. The internet is therefore the actual network whereas the world wide web (www) is the accessing of web pages using the internet.

Internet terms

Here are some important internet terms and their definitions:

Protocol – method of transferring data using the internet. A protocol is a set of rules governing the format of the data and the signals to start, control, and end the transfer of data.

HTTP (HyperText Transfer Protocol) – a protocol that defines the process of identifying, requesting, and transferring multimedia web pages over the internet.

HTTPS (HyperText Transfer Protocol secure variant) – a protocol that defines the process of identifying, requesting, and transferring multimedia web pages over the internet except unlike HTTP it uses encrypted connections to hide passwords, bank information, and other sensitive material from the open network. This is to prevent hackers from accessing and using banking details fraudulently.

Uniform Resource Locator (URL) – a web address. The system used to identify the location of a web page or document stored on the internet.

Hyperlink – a feature of a website that allows a user to jump to another web page, to jump to part of the same web page or to send an email message. Hyperlinks can be a word, phrase or image.

Internet service provider (ISP) – a company that provides users with an internet connection.

FTP (File Transfer Protocol) – a common protocol for the movement of files across the internet. Users can access a server that contains the file they want and then download it to their computer using FTP. Alternatively, they can upload a file to the server from their computer using FTP. An example of this would be when you upload your web pages to a web server where your website is hosted.

Accessing information on the internet using web browsers and search engines

Web browser – application software installed on your computer that provides a graphical user interface for accessing the internet (the HTTP protocol among others).

Search engine – application software, typically installed on a server at a company's data centre, that you access via your web browser. A search engine 'crawls' the internet, categorising and storing information about sites (metadata) so when you use your web browser to access a company's search engine to perform a search, it provides you with relevant results (for the most part).

You download and install a web browser (Google Chrome, Internet Explorer, Safari, etc.) to your computer and use it to access a search engine on the internet.

Locating information using the internet

Information on the internet can be located by:

- **Using a URL** (Uniform Resource Locator) – another name for the website address which is typed/copied into a web browser or search engine.
- **Using a search engine** – the results are displayed in order of relevance or who has paid the most to be at the top of the search.

The structure of a web address

Here is a web address: http://www.oup.com

There are several parts to this web address.

http:// stands for HyperText Transfer Protocol and this helps your web browser locate the website. You do not have to type it with some web browsers as it is added automatically.

www. stands for world wide web showing the page is on the world wide web.

oup is the name of the server or website where the website or web page is located. In many cases it will be the name of the organisation or an abbreviated version.

.com is the domain which tells you where the web page is registered and also what type of website it is. For example .com tells you that it is a commercial site. Other common domains include .org (sites for organisations), .edu (sites for schools and colleges), .ac (sites for universities), and .gov (sites for government departments). Sometimes there are suffixes such as .co.uk which tells you that the site resides in the UK. There are suffixes for most other countries as well.

Sometimes there will be a slash (/) following the domain name. For example, http://www.cie.org.uk/programmes-and-qualifications. The / followed by another word or words lets you know that you are going to a different area or page on that website.

Blogs/web logs

Blogs/web logs are online diaries of events or journals. Blogs can be about anything. Groups, singers, and celebrities have blogs which let people know about their life and what they are doing. Blogs are also used by politicians, and for collecting public opinion about certain topics.

Wikis

A wiki is a web page that can be viewed and modified by anyone who has a web browser. This means if you have web browser software then you are able to change the content of a web page. The problem with this is that you can alter the web page to post offensive messages, etc. They can be used to build up an online database of information on a certain topic or topics. An example is the encyclopaedia Wikipedia. This encyclopaedia has been created by ordinary people and anyone can add material or delete material from it.

Features of blogs and wikis:

Blogs	Wikis
A blog usually has just one author.	Wikis have many authors.
Entries are usually in reverse chronological order.	The structure is determined by the content and users.
Usually personal.	Usually objective.
Readers can add comments but are not able to edit the blog.	Contributors are able to edit entries.
Uses external links.	Both internal and external links are used.

Social networking sites

Social networking sites are online communities of people who communicate about a particular subject or interest or just make friends with others.

Using social networking sites you can:

- Create a profile with information about yourself such as school, jobs, likes, dislikes, photographs, etc.
- Search for people you have lost contact with (e.g. school or work friends).
- Invite people into your circle of friends.

The benefits of social networking sites include the following:

- Easy to keep in immediate contact with friends/make new friends.
- Easy to communicate with more than one friend/to communicate with people overseas.
- Can search for people who you've lost touch with.
- Easy to arrange meetings/visits to cinema/theatre.
- Can share photographs/videos/images/opinions/views.

The drawbacks of social networking sites include the following:

- Sites can be used to spread gossip/rumours/lies.
- Can be used for online bullying.
- Invades your privacy.
- Personal data can be given out which can put you in danger.

Advantages and disadvantages in using the internet as a source of information

Information on the internet is not always up-to-date or correct. Anyone can create a website and publish it on the internet.

Using information from the internet	
Advantages	**Disadvantages**
The information is usually more up-to-date than printed material.	The information could be unreliable.
It is quick to search for the information.	There could be too much information to read (e.g. too many hits).
It is available on your home computer and mobile devices.	It encourages students to simply copy the material rather than put it into their own words (i.e. encourages plagiarism).
You can easily obtain information from other parts of the world.	Danger of accessing inappropriate websites.

Evaluating the reliability of information on the internet

The following steps can be taken:

* Check the date that the site was last updated. Bogus sites are not updated very often. Also sites go out-of-date, so you need to be sure that the site you use has been updated recently.
* Only use sites produced by organisations you have heard of (e.g., newspapers, BBC, etc.).
* Use several sites to get the information and check that the sites are giving similar information.
* Follow the links to see if they work. Many bogus sites have links that do not work.

Exam preparation

1 The internet is a very useful source of information but the information is not always reliable.

Describe the steps you can take to check the reliability of some information you have found using the internet.

Exam-style questions

1 Give **two** benefits and **two** drawbacks of using social networking sites.

2 The internet is a useful source of information for students doing homework.

Describe the benefits and drawbacks of using the internet for doing research for homework.

Important things to remember

Fill in the missing key words

An _____ is an electronic message sent from one communication device (such as a smartphone, tablet or computer) to another using the internet. _____ are lists of people who may need to be sent the same email. There are a number of _____ which affect the way email is used. For example, in some countries emails are _____ which means other people can read their contents and then decide whether or not it should be sent to the intended recipient. You should use _____ language in your emails and not infringe _____. Many employers have _____ covering what an employee can and cannot do using email. Emails are _____ protected in order to prevent unauthorised access. When writing emails you must learn to abide by certain rules called _____ and these include such things as not using all capitals as this is considered to be 'shouting', and making sure that emails are short and to the point.

Email sent in bulk to lots of people is called _____ which clogs up your inbox and slows down the network. Spam _____ are able to recognise some email as being spam and these emails are put into a separate folder for deletion.

A web _____ is an application installed on your computer that provides you a graphical user interface for accessing the internet.

A search engine is an application typically installed on a server at a company's data centre that you access via your _____ _____.

Ways of transferring data using the internet are called _____ and these are a set of _____ governing the format of the data and the signals to start, control, and end the transfer of data.

HTTP (HyperText _____ Protocol) is a protocol that defines the process of identifying, requesting, and transferring multimedia web pages over the internet. HTTPS (HyperText Transfer Protocol secure variant) – is like HTTP except it uses _____ connections to hide passwords, bank information, and other sensitive material from the open network to prevent hackers accessing and using the data.

A uniform resource _____ (URL) is another name for a web address, and the feature of the internet that allows a user to jump to a new web page or document is called a _____.

The common protocol for moving files using the internet is called _____ _____ _____ or FTP for short.

A _____ is an online diary of events and many celebrities have them to let their fans know what they have been doing.

A _____ is a web page that can be viewed and modified by anyone who has web _____ software. This means you can add your own comments, which does cause problems as people can post _____ messages.

Social _____ sites help keep people in touch with each other and allow you to search for and find friends you have lost touch with.

1 Tick true or false next to each of these statements.

	true	false
Email groups save time if you need to send the same email to several people.		
Spam email is email from people you already know.		
Spam is a nuisance as it takes time to delete.		
Typing in all capital letters is a breach of netiquette.		
Copyright laws do not apply to the text in emails.		

2 Tick true or false next to each of these statements.

	true	false
A web browser is application software used to provide a graphical user interface for accessing web pages on the internet.		
A search engine is system software.		
A URL is a type of web browser.		
An ISP is a protocol used for transferring files using the internet.		
FTP is a protocol for the movement of files across the internet.		

3 Describe the differences between a wiki and a blog.

4 Many people use the internet as a source of information.

   A Give **two** advantages in using the internet as a source of information.

   B Give **two** disadvantages in using the internet as a source of information.

   C Explain **two** steps you can take to check that the information you obtain from the internet is accurate.

5 A school uses an intranet to which students and their parents as well as staff in the school have access.

   A Explain what is meant by the term *intranet*.

   B Describe what information the school could hold on its intranet.

   C Explain how the intranet access can be restricted to only authorised users.

Exam guidance and practice 2

What you will learn

In Paper 1 covering the theory, you can be asked questions that cover material in all the sections (i.e. 1 to 21) of the syllabus. This means, for example, you can be asked questions about spreadsheets, databases, web authoring, etc., in the theory paper.

This section of the book covers exam questions covering Sections 11 to 21 of the syllabus.

Included here are some worked examples showing sample student answers and teacher comments.

Example 1

1 Yasmin has started work after leaving university and has to live away from home. She has recorded her wages and costs into a spreadsheet and this is shown here.

	A	B	C	D	E	F	G	H	I	J
1	Month	Wages	Electricity	Gas	Phone	Rent	Clothes	Food	Total costs	Money left over
2	Jan	£1,500	£60	£55	£62	£210	£40	£600	£1,027	£473
3	Feb	£1,520	£60	£55	£65	£210	£40	£600	£1,030	£490
4	Mar	£1,550	£60	£55	£64	£210	£40	£600	£1,029	£521
5	Apr	£1,550	£60	£55	£50	£210	£40	£600	£1,015	£535
6	May	£1,680	£60	£55	£47	£210	£40	£600	£1,012	£668
7	Jun	£1,690	£60	£55	£47	£210	£40	£600	£1,012	£678
8	Jul	£1,730	£60	£55	£53	£210	£40	£600	£1,018	£712
9	Aug	£1,742	£60	£55	£54	£210	£40	£600	£1,019	£723
10	Sep	£1,800	£60	£55	£62	£210	£40	£600	£1,027	£773
11	Oct	£1,800	£60	£55	£44	£210	£40	£600	£1,009	£791
12	Nov	£1,800	£60	£55	£39	£210	£40	£600	£1,004	£796
13	Dec	£1,745	£60	£55	£53	£210	£40	£600	£1,018	£727
14										

A Which one of the following formulas could be used to work out the **Total costs** in cell **I2**?

A =SUM(I2:I13)

B =I2+I3+I4+I6+I7+I8

C = SUM(B2:H2)

D =B2+C2+D2+E2+F2+H2+I2   *(1 mark)*

B Give a suitable formula that could be entered into cell J2 to work out the money Yasmin has left over at the end of the month.

(1 mark)

C All cells (apart from cells in column A and row 1) have been formatted. Which of the following types of cell formatting have been used for these cells?

A Euros

B Calculation

C Currency

D Right align   *(1 mark)*

D Labels are important in spreadsheets. Give the cell reference of a cell containing a label.   *(1 mark)*

E Give **two** advantages of Yasmin using a spreadsheet such as this to help her budget her money.   *(2 marks)*

Sample answer 1

1 **A** D

B B2 – I2

C C

D AI

E It is quicker.

It is more efficient.

Teacher comments

1 **A** Incorrect. The destination cell (I2) should not be included in the sum.

B The student has forgotten to put the equals sign in front of this formula (i.e. =B2–I2). This is a small point but means that the answer is wrong.

C This is correct.

D A label is any cell which describes data on the spreadsheet so this is correct.

E Not a strong answer. The student needs to say in what way is it quicker and in what way is it more efficient.   *(2 marks out of 6)*

Sample answer 2

1 **A** C = SUM(B2:H2)

B =B2–I2

C C Currency

D Row I

E Provided the calculations have been set up correctly and tested, the formulas will always produce a correct calculation.

When one of the numbers in the spreadsheet is changed the cells which depend on the changed cell will recalculate automatically.

Teacher comment

1 **A** This is correct.

B This is correct.

C This is correct.

D All the cells in row 1 do contain labels but the question asks for a cell reference so this is an incorrect answer.

E These are both very good answers which give clear advantages.

(5 marks out of 6)

Teacher's suggested answer

1 **A** One mark for the letter, formula or both (i.e. C; = SUM(B2:H2))

B One mark for a correct formula which must include the equals sign (i.e. =B2–I2)

C One mark for C; Currency

D One mark for any cell reference in row 1 or column A. It must be a cell reference and not a column letter or row number.

E One mark for each of two advantages of a spreadsheet such as:
If set up correctly, the formula will always produce a correct calculation.

Automatic recalculation when numbers are changed in the spreadsheet.

Once the spreadsheet has been set up the spreadsheet can be reused for different years by putting in different data.

The data can easily be represented pictorially by using the spreadsheet to produce graphs and charts.

You can change the information in the spreadsheet in order to make and test 'what if' scenarios.

Example 2

2 A school keeps details of all its students on a computer. Part of the data is shown below. The data is structured in fields, records and files.

Student_Number	Surname	Forename	Date of birth (dd/mm/yy)	Form
1211	Lee	Jaccck	12/11/99	11T
1225	Kalmati	Aisha	34/08/09	11G

A Explain the terms:
  i Field
  ii Record
  iii File   *(3 marks)*

B The data contained in the above structure contains two mistakes. One of these mistakes could have been discovered by a verification process and the other mistake by a validation process.

Fill in the table shown below by explaining what the mistake is and whether verification or validation could have detected the mistake, and describe a method which could be used to prevent the error.

Description of mistake	Discovered by verification or validation?	Description of method which could have been used to prevent the mistake

(6 marks)

Sample answer 1

2 A i The information about a thing or person.
   ii A row in the table.
   iii The whole lot of information about a thing or person.

B

Description of mistake	Discovered by verification or validation?	Description of method which could have been used to prevent the mistake
Wrong date of birth. 34/08/09 is impossible as the days in August only go up to 31.	Validation	Range check on the days in the date to ensure it is equal to or less than 31.
Forename has wrong name entered. Jaccck should be spelled Jack.	Verification	Use a spellchecker to make sure that the name is spelled correctly.

Teacher comment

2 A i The student has defined a record here instead of a field.
   ii This answer is a bit brief but I would give one mark. A more complete answer would be to say that it is the details about a person, thing or transaction. An example would be the detail about one student which is a row in the table.
   iii This statement is a bit vague so I can't award a mark. If the student had given an example such as a collection of all the records about students in the school, then this would have been clearer.
   B The first row of answers are all correct. The last answer about a range check is okay but a data type would be better; if you allocate a data type of Date to a field then you cannot enter an impossible date.

   The second row contains a typing error and it is not appropriate to use spellcheckers with the names of people. The first two answers are correct for a mark each, but the last answer is incorrect.

(6 marks out of 9)

Sample answer 2

2 A i A field is an item of data or fact about a student. Date of birth is an example of a field.
   ii A record is a collection of fields about a person or thing. In this case it is the information about a particular student.
   iii A file is a complete collection of records and would be the complete records of every student in the school.

B	Description of mistake	Discovered by verification or validation?	Description of method which could have been used to prevent the mistake
	Incorrect date of birth 34/08/09 This is an impossible date.	Validation	Use Date format for the field. Once this is set the computer will not allow an incorrect date to be entered.
	Typing error. Jaccck should be spelt Jack.	Verification	Use a visual check. Check by reading the entered data on the screen and correct any mistakes.

Teacher comments

2 **A i** This is a good answer and notice the way the student has referred to the data in the table as an example. One mark for this.

    ii Another good answer gains another mark.

    iii Again another mark.

   B The answers to all the parts to this answer are clear and the student has used and understood the terminology. Full marks are given for this part. *(9 marks out of 9)*

Teacher's suggested answer

2 **A i** One mark for a definition such as:

    A field is an item of data such as surname, date of birth etc.

    ii One mark for a definition such as:

    A record is a collection of fields about a person or thing.

    A line in the table about one particular student is a record.

    iii One mark for a definition such as:

    A file is collection of records which forms the complete set of information about a thing or person.

    The details of all the records of all the students in a school is a file.

   B One mark for each correct answer in the table to a maximum of six marks.

Description of mistake	Discovered by verification or validation?	Description of method which could have been used to prevent the mistake
Invalid date/wrong number of days for the month/cannot have more than 31 days in a month.	Validation	Use Date format/set data type to Date. Use a range check/restrict day to 31 or less.
Typing error/transcription error. Jaccck should be Jack.	Verification	Use a visual check/ proofread/ get person who is the data subject to check their record.

Revision checklist for the practical papers

There are many skills needed for the practical papers and these can be divided into two types:

- **Generic skills** – these are skills that could be needed for any of the software you will use for the two exam papers. For example, file management, use of images, layout, styles and proofing are skills you need to apply regardless of the applications software you are using. The generic skills are extremely important as they will appear in most of the tasks you have to do.

- **Software specific skills** – these are skills that are applicable to a particular piece of applications software. For example, creating relationships would apply only to database software.

Here is a list of the skills needed for the practical examination. Use this sheet to track your progress during your revision. Photocopy the pages and tick 'Some skills' if you need to do more revision on that skill and tick 'Proficient' when you feel you have fully mastered the skill. This table will help you focus on certain areas for your revision. When all the 'Proficient' boxes are ticked you will be well prepared for the practical exams.

Syllabus reference	Skill/technique	Some skills	Proficient
11 File management			
11.1 File management	Locate stored files		
	Open/import files of different types		
	Create/save files in folder structure		
	Save and print files in different formats		
	Save and export files in different file formats (e.g. generic and non-generic)		
11.2 Reduce file sizes for storage or transmission	Reduce file sizes using compression		
12 Images			
12 Images	Place and edit an image		
	Resize an image		
	Maintain or adjust the aspect ratio of an image		
	Crop an image		
	Rotate an image		
	Reflect an image		
	Adjust the colour depth of an image		
	Adjust the brightness of an image		
	Adjust the contrast of an image		

Syllabus reference	Skill/technique	Some skills	Proficient
	Reduce image resolution to reduce file size and lower transmission speed		
13 Layout			
13 Layout	Create/open new documents/files		
	Enter text and numbers accurately		
	Manipulate text and numbers, including: highlight, delete, move, cut, copy, paste, drag and drop		
	Place objects into the document from a variety of sources, including: text, image, screen shot, spreadsheet extract, database extract, clip art or chart		
	Create a table with a specified number of rows and columns		
	Format a table and its contents		
	Place text or objects in a table		
	Wrap text around a table, chart or image, including: above, below, square and tight		
	Create headers and footers		
	Align consistently within a document the contents of the header and footer including: to left margin, right margin and centre of the page		
	Place automated objects in headers and footers, including: automated file information, automated page numbering, text, date, time		
14 Styles			
14 Styles	Produce documents which conform to a corporate house style		
	Apply styles to ensure consistency of presentation		
	Apply consistent styles using a variety of application packages		
	Ensure that page/slide layout is consistent, including: font styles, text alignment, spacing between lines, spacing between paragraphs, spacing before and after headings		
	Create and apply an appropriate style, including: font type (serif, sans-serif), point size, font colour, alignment, line spacing, style of bullets, text alignment to the left, right, centre or fully justified		
	Select an appropriate font style for a task, taking into account the audience		

Syllabus reference	Skill/technique	Some skills	Proficient
	Use text enhancement, including: bold, underline, italic, highlight		
	Create and apply paragraph style(s) with a new style name to match the corporate house style		
15 Proofing			
15.1 Software tools	Use automated tools, including spellcheck facilities, to remove errors		
	Use validation routines to minimise errors		
15.2 Proofing techniques	Correct errors in data entry, including: transposed numbers, spelling, consistent character spacing, consistent case and factual errors (following proofreading by a third party)		
	Check to ensure consistent line spacing, to remove blank pages/slides, remove widows/orphans, ensure that tables and lists are not split over columns or pages/slides		
	Visually verify data by comparison with a source of data		
	Select data to produce a graph/chart, including: using contiguous data, non-contiguous data, and specified data ranges where necessary		
16 Graphs and charts			
16 Graphs and charts	Select the graph or chart type to match the required purpose and meet the needs of the audience		
	Label the graph or chart, including: chart title, legend, sector labels, sector values, segment labels, segment values, percentages, category axis title, value axis title, category axis labels, value axis labels, scales		
	Add a second data series to a chart, as necessary		
	Add a second axis to a chart, as necessary		
	Change the maximum and minimum values of an axis scale to appropriate values		
	Enhance the appearance of a graph or chart, including: changing the colour scheme or fill patterns, extracting a pie chart sector to meet the needs of the audience		
17 Document production			
17 Document production	Set page size		
	Set page orientation		
	Set page and gutter margins		
	Set the number of columns		

Syllabus reference	Skill/technique	Some skills	Proficient
	Set the column width and spacing between columns		
	Set and remove page, section and column breaks, to adjust pagination and to avoid widows and orphans		
	Set line spacing, including: single, 1.5 times, double, multiple, spacing before and after paragraphs		
	Set tabulation settings, including: indented paragraphs, hanging paragraphs		
	Format text as bulleted or numbered lists to meet the needs of the audience		
	Edit a table structure, where necessary, to include: insert row(s), delete row(s), insert column(s), delete column(s), merge cells		
	Set horizontal cell alignment: left, right, centre, fully justified		
	Set vertical cell alignment: top, centre, bottom		
	Format cells and the cell contents, including: show gridlines, hide gridlines, wrap text within a cell, shading/colouring cells		
	Edit a master document to insert appropriate fields from a data source		
	Insert special fields, such as date		
	Select records to merge		
	Merge a document with selected fields		
	Save and print merge master document		
	Save and print selected merged documents as appropriate		
	Assign appropriate data types to fields, including: text, numeric, (integer, decimal, percentage, currency), date/time, Boolean/logical (1/0, yes/no, true/false)		
18 Creating a database structure			
18.1 Create a database structure	Format fields and identify sub-types, including: specifying the number of decimal places, specifying a particular currency		
	Locate, open and import data from an existing file		
	Create a relationship between two or three tables		
	Create a data entry form to meet the needs of the audience		
	Create a data entry form with all fields included to match the purpose of the task		

Syllabus reference	Skill/technique	Some skills	Proficient
	Create an appropriate data entry form, including: appropriate font styles and sizes, spacing between fields, character spacing of individual fields, use of white space, radio buttons, drop-down menus, highlighting key fields		
	Create a calculated field		
18.2 Manipulate data	Perform calculations at run time using formulae and functions, including: addition, subtraction, multiplication, division, sum, average, maximum, minimum, count		
	Sort data using a single criterion and using multiple criteria where necessary, into ascending or descending order		
	Perform suitable searches using a single criterion and using multiple criteria, on different field types like alphanumeric, numeric, Boolean		
	Perform searches using a variety of operators including: AND, OR, NOT, LIKE, >, <, =, >=, <=, <>		
	Perform searches using wildcards		
	Produce reports to display all the required data and labels in full where required		
18.3 Present data	Use appropriate headers and footers within a database report, including: report header, report footer, page header, page footer		
	Set report titles		
	Produce different output layouts as required, including: tabular format, labels		
	Align data and labels appropriately, including: right aligning numeric data and decimal alignment		
	Format numeric data, including: number of decimal places, variety of currencies, percentages as required by the task		
	Show and hide data and labels within a report		
	Export data for use in another application		
	Use the master slide to place objects appropriately, including: images, text, logos, slide footers, automated slide numbering		

Syllabus reference	Skill/technique	Some skills	Proficient
19 Presentations			
19 Presentations	Use the master slide to set font styles, heading styles and colour schemes as required by the audience		
	Manipulate and use specified areas for headings, subheadings, bullets, images, charts, colours, text boxes, presenter notes, audience notes as appropriate		
	Insert a new slide, when required, selecting the appropriate slide type for the purpose		
	Place text on the slides including: headings, subheadings, bulleted lists where appropriate		
	Apply consistent styles using available software tools, including: select from the presentation colour scheme, the use of text enhancement		
	Place appropriate images on the slides, including: still images, video clips, animated images		
	Place sound within a slide		
	Place charts imported from a spreadsheet		
	Place other objects including: symbols, lines, arrows, call out boxes		
	Create consistent transitions between pages		
	Create consistent animation facilities on text, images and other objects		
	Use suitable software tools to display the presentation in a variety of formats, including: looped on-screen carousel, controlled presentation, presenter notes, audience notes taking into account the needs of the audience		
	Enter data with 100% accuracy		
20 Create a data model			
20.1 Create a data model	Edit the structure of an existing model, including: inserting cells, deleting cells, inserting rows, deleting rows, inserting columns, deleting columns		
	Use mathematical operators, including: add, subtract, multiply, divide, indices, where necessary		
	Use absolute and relative references, named cells, named ranges and nested formulae, as appropriate		
	Use functions, including: sum, average, maximum, minimum, integer, rounding, counting, LOOKUP, VLOOKUP, HLOOKUP, IF and nested functions, when necessary		

Syllabus reference	Skill/technique	Some skills	Proficient
	Test the model, correcting errors and re-testing, where appropriate		
20.2 Test the data model	Test the model by the use of what ifs		
	Search using a single criterion and using multiple criteria, where appropriate, with a variety of operators like: AND, OR, NOT, LIKE, >, <, =, >=, <=		
20.3 Manipulate data	Search, where appropriate, using wildcards		
	Sort data using a single criterion and using multiple criteria into ascending or descending order, as required		
	Adjust row height, column width and cell sizes so that all data, labels, and formulae are fully visible		
20.4 Present data	Wrap text within cells so that all data are fully visible		
	Hide and display rows and columns, where appropriate		
	Use features to enhance a spreadsheet, including: text colour, cell colour, bold, underline, italic and shading to meet the needs of the audience		
	Format numeric data to display the number of decimal places, a variety of different currency values, percentages as appropriate		
	Set the spreadsheet to display formulae and values		
	Set the page orientation to portrait or landscape as necessary		
	Set the page layout so that it prints on a specified number of pages		
	Use conditional formatting appropriately to change the display format depending upon the contents of a cell		
21 Website authoring			
21.1 Web development layers	Use software tools to create the content layer of a web page		
21.2 Create a web page	Insert a table, including: table header, table rows, table data		
	Use attributes within a table, including: width in terms of pixels and % values, border to create visible and invisible borders, set the border thickness, merging cells, background colour, horizontal alignment, vertical alignment, to meet the needs of the audience		

Syllabus reference	Skill/technique	Some skills	Proficient
	Insert appropriate objects into a web page including: text, still images, moving images, sound clips		
	Apply styles to text within a web page		
	Apply styles to a list, including: ordered list, unordered list		
	Insert an appropriate image into a web page		
	Use appropriate attributes of an image to adjust its size		
	Create an anchor within a web page		
	Create hyperlinks from: text, images		
	Create hyperlinks, where appropriate, to: anchors on the same page, other locally stored web pages, a website using the URL, send mail to a specified email address, open in a specified location including: the same window, new window, with a window named as specified		
	Create generic external styles including: background properties (like colour), table properties (like border, spacing, padding), font properties (like style, typeface)		
21.3 Use stylesheets	Create external styles to be tagged in a web page including: h1, h2, h3, p, li as required		
	Specify the font appearance for each style, including features like: font family, size, colour, alignment, bold and italic		
	Save styles in cascading stylesheet format		
	Attach an external stylesheet to a web page using a relative file path		
	Upload and publish the content of a website using ftp		
21.4 Publish a website	Test that web page elements work		
	Test navigation within/from a web page using a test plan		
	Create a test plan to test a website including: web page elements are visible, navigation within/from a web page		

Theoretical knowledge needed for Paper 1

You can be tested on the theory behind any of the work you do in the practical papers (i.e. Papers 2 and 3) and in the theory paper (Paper 1). For example, you could be asked to explain the difference between relative and absolute cell referencing or asked about why files are often compressed.

To help with your revision, here is a list of theory, definitions and explanations which can be asked for in the theory paper.

Use this sheet to track your progress during your revision. Photocopy the pages and tick 'Limited/No knowledge' if you need to do more revision and tick 'Proficient' when you feel you have fully mastered the theory. This table will help you focus on certain areas for your revision. When all the 'Proficient' boxes are ticked you will be well prepared for the practical exams.

Syllabus reference	Content	Limited/No knowledge	Proficient
11 File management			
11.1 File management	Identify different file types and their use/s, for example: css, csv, gif, htm, jpg, pdf, png, rtf, txt, zip		
	Explain why generic file formats are needed		
11.2 Reduce file sizes for storage or transmission	Explain the need to reduce file sizes for storage or transmission		
	Identify where it will be necessary to reduce file sizes for storage or transmission		
12 Images			
12 Images	Understand the need to reduce image resolution to increase transmission speed		
13 Layout			
13 Layout	Explain why headers and footers are needed		
14 Styles			
14 Styles	Understand the purpose of a corporate house style		
	Explain what is meant by a corporate branding/house style		
	Explain why consistency of presentation is needed		
	Explain the difference between a serif and a sans serif font		
15 Proofing			
15.1 Software tools	Explain why the automated suggestions given by spellcheck software do not always give the correct response		
	Explain why validation checks must be appropriate to the data that is being checked		

Syllabus reference	Content	Limited/No knowledge	Proficient
15.2 Proofing techniques	Describe the importance of accuracy and the potential consequences of data entry errors		
	Define the term *verification*		
	Describe visual verification (i.e. visual comparison of data entered with a data source)		
	Describe double data entry (i.e. entering data twice and the computer compares the two sets of data, either by comparing them after data has been entered or by comparing them during data entry)		
	Explain the need for validation as well as verification		
16 Graphs and charts			
16 Graphs and charts	Select the graph or chart type to match the required purpose and meet the needs of the audience		
17 Document production			
17 Document production	Define the terms *widow* and *orphan*		
	Explain why it is necessary to use page, section and column breaks, to adjust pagination and to avoid widows and orphans		
	Explain why mail-merged documents are created		
	Explain the need for validation as well as verification		
18 Data manipulation			
18.1 Create a database structure	Define the terms *flat-file database* and *relational database*		
	Explain where it would be appropriate to select a flat-file database or a relational database		
	Assign appropriate data types to fields, including: text, numeric, (integer, decimal, percentage, currency), date/time, Boolean/logical (1/0, yes/no, true/false)		
	Explain that other field types like placeholders for media, including images, sound bites and video clips are used in commercial databases		
	Define and understand the terms *primary key* and *foreign key* and their role in a relational database		
	Discuss the advantages and disadvantages of using relational tables rather than a flat-file database		
	Understand the key features of form design		

Syllabus reference	Content	Limited/No knowledge	Proficient
18.2 Manipulate data	Understand the difference between a formula and a function		
	Constructing formulae correctly		
19 Presentations			
19 Presentations	Identify the need for consistency of presentation, in terms of styles, point sizes, colour schemes, transitions and animations		
20 Data analysis			
20.1 Create a data model	Define the terms: *cells, rows, columns, sheets, tabs, pages, charts*		
	Explain the importance of accurate data entry in spreadsheets		
	Define the terms: *formula, function, absolute reference, relative reference, ranges, named cell, named range, nested formulae/functions*		
	Explain the difference between a formula and a function		
	Use mathematical operators, including: add, subtract, multiply, divide, indices, where necessary		
	Explain the function , and use, of absolute and relative referencing, as appropriate, when formulae are to be replicated		
20.2 Test the data model	Define the terms: *testing, test data, expected outcome, actual outcome, normal data, abnormal data, extreme data, 'what if'*		
	Explain the need to test a model before it is used		
	Select appropriate test data to thoroughly test a data model and justify the choice of test data		
20.3 Manipulate data	Use of operators for searching such as AND, OR, NOT, LIKE, >, <, =, >=, <=		
	Use of wildcards		
21 Website authoring			
21.1 Web development layers	Identify and describe the three web development layers		
	Understand the function of: content layer to enter the content of a web page structure; presentation layer to format whole web page(s) or individual elements; behaviour layer to enter scripting language to a web page or an individual element		

Syllabus reference	Content	Limited/No knowledge	Proficient
21.2 Create a web page	Explain why tables are used to structure elements within a web page		
	Describe the function of a hyperlink		
	Describe the function of an anchor and why it is rarely seen from the browser view		
	Define and understand the terms *relative file path* and *absolute file path*		
	Explain why absolute file paths must not be used for hyperlinks to locally saved web pages/objects		
21.3 Use stylesheets	Explain what is meant by the term *cascading stylesheets*		
	Explain the hierarchy of multiple attached stylesheets and in-line styles within a web page		
	Explain why relative file paths must be used for attached stylesheets		
21.4 Test and publish a website	Create a test plan to test a website including: web page elements are visible, navigation within/from a web page		
	Justify the choice of test plan		

Exam guidance and practice 3

What you will learn

Before taking your final examinations, it is important to **take stock of your knowledge** and **check your understanding** of the IGCSE course in ICT.

In this section there is a practice exam-style paper, covering the Theory elements of the course. To practise the practical papers, you are best using the papers your teacher will give you or those on the CIE website.

Use the **techniques** you have learned in this book to answer the questions and **identify any gaps** in your understanding.

Ask your parents, guardians or teachers to time each paper and then to help you mark your answers and suggest how to improve them if necessary.

How to prepare for your final examinations in ICT

Final checklist

- Read through all the **Revision Summaries** at the start of each unit to check your understanding of key ICT concepts and terms.
- Read the **Important Things to Remember** page at the end of each unit.
- Quickly study the **top tips and techniques** covered in the Exam Guidance and Practice sections 1 and 2.
- If time has run out for further revision, don't worry and don't hurriedly learn any new topics. Just concentrate on what you already know.
- Do not stay up all night revising before an exam paper. You will perform better if you sleep well.

Top tips for the exam

The following list gives some hints on things you should do when actually taking the exam:

1 Always read the instructions on the front of the paper carefully. In particular, note the time you are allowed.
2 Time yourself. Don't spend too much time on a question that you can answer well at the expense of other questions.
3 Try to write neatly. The examiners have hundreds of scripts to mark and do not have time to decipher your untidy script.
4 Only do what the question asks. If it asks for two reasons, make sure that you give two: not three or one. Always check that, in an answer to a question with two parts, you have not written similar answers to both parts.
5 Use the mark scheme at the side of the questions as a guide to how much you should write.
6 After you have answered a question, read the question through again to make sure that you have not missed out part of it.

Working through question papers

You now have the chance to work through a practice exam-style paper.

Before taking the paper:

- Plan a time to take the practice exam-style paper.
- Find a quiet room and ask a parent, guardian or teacher to time you on each paper and enforce exam conditions (i.e. talking and looking at your notes are not permitted).

Sample answers are supplied at the end of the book. Check your own answers against these or ask your teacher to help you mark your papers.

Paper 1 Theory: 2 hours

Answer **all** questions.

1 Name the storage media A, B, C and D using words from the list.

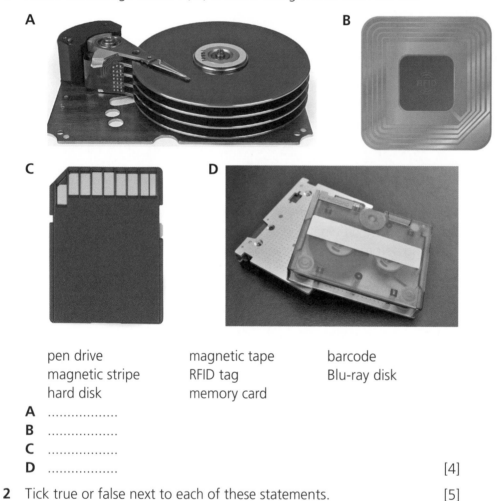

A

B

C

D

pen drive	magnetic tape	barcode
magnetic stripe	RFID tag	Blu-ray disk
hard disk	memory card	

A ....

B ....

C ....

D ....   [4]

2 Tick true or false next to each of these statements.   [5]

	true	false
Antivirus programs are examples of hardware.		
A keyboard is an example of an external hardware device.		
Apps or applets are examples of software.		
Video cards are external hardware devices.		
Linkers are part of the systems software.		

3 Circle **three** items which are classed as direct data entry devices.   [3]
keyboard   pen drive   mouse   magnetic stripe reader
joystick   internal hard disk   portable hard disk
chip and PIN reader   barcode reader   trackerball

4 Tick **internet** or **world wide web** next to each statement as
appropriate.   [4]

	internet	world wide web
Is a means of accessing information		
Consists of computer hardware		
Is a huge network of networks		
Uses http and web browsers to access information		

5 Schools use ICT to remove some of their administrative burden. For
example, registering pupil attendance can be done using ICT rather
than by using a paper-based register where the form teacher would
record attendance.
   A Describe **three** different methods by which ICT systems can be
   used to record pupil attendance.   [6]
   B Give **two** advantages in using ICT systems to record and process
   pupil attendance details.   [2]

6 The manager of a tool hire company wishes to use a relational database
to help keep track of the business. The database stores the data in
three tables, namely: Tools, Customers and Rentals.
   A Explain what a relational database is and describe what its
   main features are.   [5]
   B Explain the main advantages to **this** manager in storing the
   data in a relational database rather than a flat-file database.   [3]

7 Graphical user interfaces (GUIs) are a feature of the software on most
computers.
   A Explain why a computer needs a user interface.   [2]
   B Give **one** input device, other than a keyboard, that can be used
   with a graphical user interface.   [1]
   C Give **four** features of a graphical user interface.   [4]
   D **i** Give **one** other type of user interface.   [1]
      ii Give **two** benefits to an inexperienced user offered by a
      graphical user interface compared with this type of interface.   [2]

8 A software developer is working as part of a team of ten developers
who are developing new software for an online loans company. The
team members work in different parts of the country.

The developers need to keep in touch with each other and need to pass
work (mainly programs, screen designs, etc.) to each other.
   A Explain **three** advantages of the developers contacting each
   other by email rather than by post.   [6]
   B Describe **two** facilities provided by email software that will
   make it a lot easier to work as a team.   [4]

9   An examination is marked out of 50. The highest mark a student can obtain is 50 and the lowest is 0.

The system for recording these marks is to be tested using a test plan which makes use of normal data, abnormal data and extreme data.

A   Give the meanings of the terms
   i   normal data
   ii   abnormal data
   iii extreme data.   [3]
B   Give **two** items of extreme data that could be used to test this system.   [2]

10 A small business intends to network six computers together to form a small cabled LAN. A friend of the owner has suggested that they should use a WLAN.

A   Explain the difference between a cabled LAN and a WLAN.   [2]
B   Give **two** advantages and **two** disadvantages in using a WLAN rather than a LAN for the network.   [4]
C   It is important that only authenticated users are allowed access to the network.

Give **two** different methods of authenticating a user.   [2]

11 A floor turtle uses the following set of instructions:

INSTRUCTION	MEANING
FORWARD *n*	Move *n* forward
BACKWARD *n*	Move *n* backward
LEFT *t*	Turn left *t* degrees
RIGHT *t*	Turn right *t* degrees
PENUP	Lift the pen
PENDOWN	Lower the pen
REPEAT *n*	Repeat the following instructions *n* times
END REPEAT	Finish the REPEAT loop

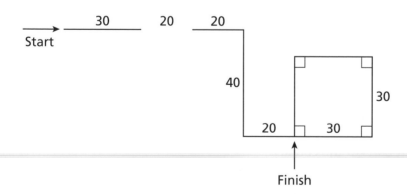

Complete the following set of instructions to draw the shape shown by filling in the blank lines provided. The pen is UP at the start. You must not add additional lines.

PENDOWN
FORWARD 30

_____

_____

PENDOWN

_____

_____

FORWARD 40

_____

FORWARD 20
LEFT 90

_____

_____

_____

_____   [9]

12 Most countries have data protection laws which protect personal information stored on computers from being misused.
   A Give **two** items of personal information that would be covered by a data protection law.   [2]
   B Give **two** rights given to an individual by a data protection law. [2]
   C Describe examples of situations that could be caused by incorrect information being held about a person.   [4]

13 Encryption is used to make data secure.
   A Describe what is meant by encryption.   [4]
   B Discuss the benefits and drawbacks of using encryption.   [4]

14 A car factory has introduced robots to the production line for manufacturing cars.

   Discuss the advantages and disadvantages of introducing robots to the production line in a car factory.   [6]

15 A car hire company keeps records of all its cars in a database. Part of this database is shown below:

Vehicle_ID	Make	Model	Number_of_doors	Air_conditioning
091101Y	Volkswagen	Golf	4	Y
020099Y	Fiat	Punto	2	N
100112X	Nissan	Micra	2	Y
109871Z	Audi	A3	2	Y

   A Explain what is meant by the term *primary key* and give the name of the field that should be used as the primary key.   [2]
   B i   Give the fieldname of the field that stores Boolean data.
      ii Give the reason for using this data type for this field.   [2]
   C i   Give the fieldname of the field that stores numeric data.
      ii Give the reason for using this data type for this field.   [2]

16 A hospital is planning to build an expert system that can be used by doctors to improve the diagnosis of certain illnesses.

Describe the steps that need to be taken in order to build this expert system. [5]

17 A business has lots of branches throughout the world. In the past, the managers of these branches had to attend a meeting in London twice a year but now the business uses video-conferencing rather than face-to-face meetings.

Discuss the advantages and disadvantages of using video-conferencing rather than face-to-face meetings. [8]

18 The internet can be accessed using a variety of devices such as smartphones, tablets, laptops and desktops.

Compare and contrast the use of each of these devices to access the internet. [6]

Answers

Chapter 1

Exam preparation

1 **A** A desktop is much larger/heavier.

A desktop usually has a larger screen.

A desktop consists of separate components whereas a laptop has all the components built in.

A desktop uses the mains power only whereas laptops can use mains or battery power.

A desktop uses a mouse where laptops usually use a touch pad.

It is easier to repair and upgrade a desktop.

B A laptop has a physical keyboard whereas tablets use on-screen keyboards.

Laptops are hard to use whilst standing up whereas tablets are easy to use standing up.

Laptops are generally heavier than tablets so less portable.

Laptops sometimes use a touch screen but tablets always use them.

Laptops have optical drives; Tablets do not have optical drives.

C Tablets are larger than smartphones so less portable.

The screen is larger on a tablet making it easier to use.

Tablets are harder to use on the move compared to a smartphone.

Tablets have a larger on-screen keyboard which makes typing easier.

Exam-style questions

1 **A** Hardware – are the physical components of a computer system (i.e. the parts you can physically touch such as keyboard, mouse, monitor/screen, etc.).

Software – are programs for controlling the operation of the computer or the processing of electronic data.

B Internal – motherboard, ROM and RAM, internal hard disk, video card, sound card.

External – screen/monitor, keyboard, mouse, printer, scanner, speakers, portable hard disk drive, etc.

C
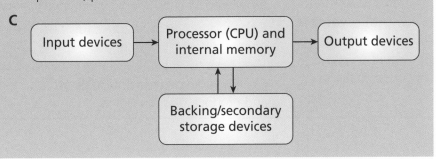

2 A Two answers such as:

Full-sized keyboard makes typing search criteria easier.

Large screen means less scrolling and easier to see the web pages.

Usually a cabled connection to the internet which is faster and more reliable.

B Two answers such as:

You can't move around whilst using a desktop.

Needs a mains power supply.

Cannot fit in your pocket like a smartphone so this limits its availability.

Important things to remember

Computer systems consist of physical components you can touch called **hardware** and the instructions, data and programs to tell the computer what to do called **software**.

Hardware inside the computer casing (such as the motherboard, RAM and ROM) is called **internal** hardware and hardware outside the computer casing (such as keyboards and printers) are called **external** hardware.

Software used to control the computer hardware directly is called **system** software, and that used to accomplish as task such as word proccessing is called **applications** software.

Device driver software gives instructions to the computer as to how to use a new hardware device such as a new printer attached to the computer.

Operating systems, linkers and compilers are examples of **system** software.

The central processing unit is the brain of the computer and it carries out the instructions given to it by the hardware and **software**.

There are two types of internal memory: ROM and **RAM**. The BIOS program used to start the computer is stored in **ROM** which is non-volatile meaning it retains its contents when the power is removed. RAM is **volatile** meaning it loses its contents when the power is removed, and it is used to hold program instructions and user data currently being worked on.

Secondary/backing storage is slower storage and includes the internal hard disk as well as external hard disk, pen drives, tape drives, etc.

Operating systems require an **interface** to allow a user to communicate with them and there are two main types: a graphical user interface and a **command line** interface. A GUI consists of windows, **icons**, **menus** and pointers and uses a mouse or touch pad to make selections. A command line interface works by the user typing in carefully constructed **commands/instructions** and this makes it hard to use.

There are a number of **biometric** methods used to recognise a person to allow them access to buildings, countries or computer resources. One method called **retinal** scanning uses the unique pattern of blood vessels at the back of the eye and another method called **iris** scanning uses the pattern on the coloured area around the pupil to recognise a person. Another method called **fingerprinting** uses the unique pattern on a finger or thumb to recognise a person.

Other emerging technologies include using quantum physics for quantum **cryptography** which allows very secure transmission of secret information, and **vision** enhancement, which can allow partially blind people to improve their sight.

Robots are used in factories for the assembly of components, welding, paint-spraying, etc. They have the advantages that they don't need paying, can work **continuously** without a break and produce high-quality work.

1

	true	false
A graphical user interface is a method of interacting with a user.	✔	
A compiler is an example of system software.	✔	
A laptop computer is usually larger than a desktop computer.		✔
An icon is part of a command line interface.		✔
Input devices are examples of hardware.	✔	

	true	false
One disadvantage in using GUIs is that older computers may need to be upgraded owing to their increased memory and processor requirements.	✔	
Biometric devices are computers that behave like the human brain.		✔
Graphical user interfaces have features such as windows, icons, menus and pointers.	✔	

2

	true	false
System software is a set of programs and not a single program.	✔	
Command line interfaces are usually considered to be the easiest interface to use.		✔

3 See the table in Section 1.2 page 10.

4 A Two such as: welding car panels, paint spraying, moving components around, assembling components.

   B See the table in Section 1.5 page 12.

5 See table in Section 1.3 page 10.

6 See Section 1.5 page 11.

Chapter 2

Exam preparation

1 A i Magnetic stripe reader

    ii Joystick

    iii Touch screen

    iv Barcode reader

    v Mouse

  B i Inkjet printer

    ii Laser printer

    iii Dot matrix printer

Exam-style questions

1

	true	false
Dot matrix printers produce high quality output.		✔
Inkjet printers are a lot noisier than dot matrix printers.		✔
Wide format printers are used when very large hard copy is needed.	✔	
Inkjet printers always use continuous stationery.		✔
Laser printers are usually much faster than inkjet printers.	✔	

2 See table in Section 2.2 page 21.

3 A The data is contained on a machine-readable card or form so the data can be input directly into the computer by the input device.

B Magnetic stripe readers, chip readers and PIN pads, RFID readers, magnetic ink character readers (MICR), optical character readers (OCR), barcode readers.

Important things to remember

Input devices are used to enter data and **instructions** into the computer for processing. **Keyboards** come with most computers and can be physical or on-screen. Pointing devices are used to make selections using a GUI and these can be mice or **touch pads**. **Trackerballs** which are like upside down mice, can also be used to make selections.

Numeric keypads are smaller than ordinary keyboards and usually just contain numbers and are used with chip and **PIN** for entering personal identification numbers when using a credit/debit card.

Other input devices include **remote** controls for controlling devices such as TVs at a distance and **joysticks** for playing computer games.

A **touch screen** is an input device that detects the presence and location when a screen is touched and is found with tablet computers and smartphones.

Larger input devices include **scanners** which can be used to digitise documents and old photographs. When used with special **OCR** software, it is possible for the scanned text to be recognised as individual letters so that they can be input into a word-processed document. **Digital** cameras are input devices and can be bought separately or combined in tablet computers and smartphones and the images are easily stored in the cloud for access from any device with internet access. **Microphones** are input devices that allow speech to be recorded, or for verbal instructions to be given to the operating system to accomplish tasks. Such systems use voice **recognition** and are fairly accurate provided the person speaks clearly and there is no background noise.

Sensors such as those measuring pressure, temperature, light and humidity/moisture are used to input signals in control systems. In these systems, the processor decides what action should be taken by the **output** devices.

Video cameras are **input** devices that capture both still and moving images and are now built into tablet computers and smartphones.

Web cams can be used to input live video images and this in conjunction with a microphone allows you to conduct conversations using the internet where you can see the person you are talking to.

There is a range of input devices called **direct** data entry devices where data is input directly from a form or a card into the computer for processing. Direct data entry devices include **magnetic** stripe readers, chip readers and **PIN** pads, RFID readers, magnetic **ink character** readers, optical **mark** readers, barcode readers and **optical** character readers.

Screens/monitors are the most popular **output** device as they are part of every computer system or smartphone. **CRT** monitors are the large, heavy and now old-fashioned monitors that have been replaced by the thin and lighter **TFT/LCD** screens that are used with most desktop and laptop computers. The **radiation** given off by a LCD screen is much less than that produced by a CRT monitor and the heat given off is

also much less. In-plane switching, or **IPS** for short, is a type of LCD screen which has a faster response time to fast-moving images and where there is a greater viewing angle allowing more people to view the screen at the same time.

Another type of monitor is the **LED** monitor which is very light compared to CRT monitors and uses much less power which is why they are used in portable devices which are powered by rechargeable batteries.

If the output from the screen needs to be viewed by a lot of people then a **multimedia** projector can be used to project the image from a computer onto a large screen. When projected onto a large screen the image **quality** is not as good and the projector needs to be used in a darkened room.

Speakers and headphones/earphones are **output** devices used to output speech/sounds and music. Output devices used as output from **control** systems include motors, buzzers, lamps and heaters.

10 MINUTE TEST

1

	true	false
A laser printer and a motor are both examples of output devices.	✔	
Sensors are output devices.		✔
A pressure sensor is used to send data to a processor in a washing machine.	✔	
A dot matrix printer uses continuous stationery.	✔	
Speakers are input devices.		✔

2

	true	false
A touch screen is both an input and output device.	✔	
A wide format printer is used to print large maps and plans.	✔	
An inkjet printer is usually noisier than a dot matrix printer.		✔
OMR can be used to read data from multiple-choice answer sheets.	✔	
OCR is used to read the data on bank cheques.		✔

3 A Dot matrix printer
   B Wide format printer
   C 3D printer
   D Dot matrix printer
   E Wide format printer
   F Inkjet printer
   G 3D printer

4 A Magnetic stripe reader
   B Optical mark reader
   C RFID reader
   D Magnetic ink character reader

5 See Section 2.3, page 22.

6 **Advantages**
   A RFID tag can hold more information about books and borrowers compared to a barcode.

RFID tags can be read at a distance so can read details if membership card or books are in your bag. These both need to be taken out if a barcode is used.

Can return books when the library is closed as the tags on the books can be read at a distance unlike barcodes.

Disadvantages

RFID tags are expensive to produce compared to barcodes.

RFID readers are more expensive than a barcode reader.

There is the danger that hackers can access the radio signals used. This cannot happen with a barcode reader.

Chapter 3

Exam preparation

1 A **Advantages**
      Fixed hard disk has a higher storage capacity than an optical disk.

      The time it takes to find data/access speed is lower for a fixed hard disk.

      The transfer rate for reading/writing data is higher for a fixed hard disk.

      Disadvantages
      Fixed hard disks are not removable but optical disks are, which makes optical disks suitable for taking backup copies.

      Fixed hard disks are cannot be used to move files between computers as they are not removable like optical disks.

   B **Advantages**
      Portable hard disks have higher storage capacities compared to pen drives.

      The access speed is higher for a portable hard disk.

      The transfer rate is higher for a portable hard disk.

      Portable hard disks are larger so they are less likely to be left in the machine like a pen drive.

      Disadvantages
      Portable hard disks are not pocket sized so are not as transportable.

      Not as durable, as pen drives are solid state so do not have moving parts.

   C **Advantages**
      High access speed (i.e. finding data).

      Can access data directly whereas a tape has to be wound/rewound to find a file.

Disadvantages

No use for backup as fixed hard disk cannot be removed for security purposes.

Hard disk is not as fast compared to a tape for storing/reading data when all the data has to be saved/read.

Exam-style questions

1 A Advantages

Desktop computer has a full-sized keyboard which makes typing easier.

Desktop computers usually have cabled connection to the internet which is faster than using wireless.

Larger screen means reading text is much easier.

The full version of a website can be used whereas smartphones often use trimmed versions which do not include all the features.

B Disadvantages

Desktop computers are not portable so cannot be used whilst on the move.

Desktop computers usually use a cabled internet connection so you are restricted to using the internet at a desk.

You cannot use a desktop whilst walking but you can use the smartphone.

Important things to remember

The material on which data and programs are stored is called the storage **media** and the device doing the recording is called the storage **device**. Backing storage is not as fast as internal memory but it is cheaper and, unlike RAM, it does not lose its contents when there is no power. Backing storage is defined as storage other than **ROM** and RAM which is non-volatile and is used to hold **data/programs** not being used.

Magnetic storage media stores data as a **magnetic** pattern on the storage media which is usually hard disk or **tape**. Hard disks have a high **access** speed, a high transfer rate and a very high **storage** capacity. **Fixed** hard disks cannot be removed from the computer whereas **portable** hard disks can be.

Magnetic tapes have a huge storage capacity and are ideal for backing up data stored on large hard disks such as those used as **servers** for networks. They are suitable when all the data and programs on the hard disk need to be **copied** but are unsuitable when **fast** access to data is needed.

Optical disks store data as a series of bumps on a plastic disk which reflect laser light. CD ROM is **read-only** and is used to store programs and music. DVD ROM is also read-only and has a larger **storage** capacity compared to CD ROM and is used to store movies. CD R and DVD R can have data **recorded** onto them but only once but **CD RW** allows the CD to have data recorded onto them by the user many times. DVD RW drives can be used to read as well as **store** data and the newer DVD RAM are much faster at reading and writing data.

Blu-ray disks have a higher storage capacity than those mentioned previously and are used for the storage of movies in **high** definition.

Solid **state** backing storage devices have no moving parts and are small and reliable, although their storage capacities are **lower/smaller/less**. They have lower **access** speeds compared to hard disks and are small so they are easily lost or stolen. They include **memory** cards and memory sticks or **pen** drives and are ideal for transferring small files between computers.

10 MINUTE TEST

1 Memory stick, Magnetic tape drive, Portable hard disk drive and DVD RAM drive.

2

	true	false
Magnetic hard disk drives are always portable.		✔
An optical disk which can have data updated is DVD RW.	✔	
Fixed hard disks are unsuitable for taking backup copies.	✔	
Solid state backing storage includes magnetic tape.		✔
Blu-ray disks have a larger storage capacity than DVD.	✔	

3 **A** A copy of programs or data kept on removable media or in the cloud for security purposes in case the originals are damaged or destroyed.

B i If the computer was stolen or destroyed, if the backup was stored on the same computer then both the original and backup data would be lost. It needs to be on removable media that can be removed away from the original data.

ii Advantages of portable magnetic hard disk
Easy to attach to the USB port.
Fast transfer rate of data and programs.
Small and portable means they are easily taken off the premises.
Disadvantages of portable magnetic hard disk
Small size means they are easily lost or stolen.
Slower than magnetic tape for copying lots of data (e.g. all the data off a server).
Advantages of magnetic tape
Very fast at copying large amounts of data and programs.

Much higher storage capacity compared to magnetic hard disk.
Disadvantages of magnetic tape
Drives are more expensive compared to magnetic hard disk drives.
Only suitable when all the files need copying.

4

	true	false
Fixed hard disk and portable hard disk are both examples of magnetic media.	✔	
Memory cards are examples of magnetic media.		✔
Memory cards are thin cards used mainly in cameras for storing photographs.	✔	
Memory cards cannot be removed from the camera.		✔
Magnetic tape can be used for taking backup copies of data stored on servers.	✔	

5 **A** Both these storage devices can have data written to them and they are both removable so they can be stored away from the building/computer in case the computer containing the original data is stolen, damaged or destroyed.

B Solid state backing storage has no moving parts and is durable.
Hard disk has a higher storage capacity.
Solid state backing storage has a lower access speed.
Solid state backing storage is silent in operation.
Solid state backing storage does not use magnetic media.

C i Pen drives/memory sticks.
ii Transferring small numbers of files between computers.

Chapter 4

Exam preparation

1 Use a system of usernames and passwords that have to be entered to allow access to the network. Only if both are entered correctly will the user be allowed access. Passwords should be changed regularly so if they become known by hackers, they can only be used for a short time.

Use firewalls to prevent hackers accessing computers using the internet. The firewall is able to detect attempts to access the computer using the internet and can block the illegal access.

Use biometric methods such as fingerprinting, retinal scanning or iris recognition to only allow authorised access. The system compares the information to that stored by the system to see if there is a match.

Exam-style question

1 **A** Most websites are designed to be viewed on a desktop computer so it will appear as the designer intended.

The screens are larger so you will not need to scroll the text to see it all.

Easier to type in search conditions using a full-sized keyboard.

Usually faster internet access as they generally use cables rather than WiFi to connect to the internet.

B Desktops cannot normally be used away from mains power.

They are too large to be used when on the move.

Generally use a wired/cabled internet connection so you are restricted by the length of the wire/cable.

Important things to remember

Networks are two or more computers linked together so that they can share resources such as printers, an internet connection, software and data. **Network** devices are needed to build a network and these can include **routers** that read address information to determine the final destination of packets of data and can connect networks so they are able to share a single **internet** connection. Network **interface** cards are needed which connect the motherboard to an external socket into which network cables can be connected. **Hubs** and switches are used to connect devices in a network but a switch is more intelligent as it **inspects** packets of data to check they are being forwarded to the correct computer.

There are other network devices such as **bridges** used to connect local area networks together and **modems** which convert digital data into sound and vice versa so that telephone lines can be used to transmit data.

Wireless communication between computers and other devices can be achieved using **Bluetooth** or WiFi and the former is used over **short** distances and where slow bandwidth is acceptable.

Once the computers and other network devices have been connected or linked you need an **ISP/ internet service provider** to provide you with an internet connection as to have one yourself is very **expensive**.

You then need **browser/web browser** software to allow web pages stored on the internet to be viewed. The internet is a huge **network** of networks and the **world wide web** is a way of accessing the information on these networked computers.

Internal networks can also make use of internet technology and these are called **intranets**. These networks hold information that is used by an organisation and sometimes their trading partners and they are protected using authentication techniques such as **passwords**.

There are two types of network; a LAN and a **WAN**. LANs are confined to a **small** area and use communication links that are usually owned by the organisation. WANs cover wide areas, often over different countries and use communication equipment such as satellites which are **not** owned by the organisation.

LANs are often **wireless** in which case they are called WLANs.

There are many security issues with networks including **password** interception, **virus** attack and **hackers** accessing information illegally. To prevent unauthorised access a **firewall** is used to block outgoing or incoming data if it is suspect.

Access to computers can be controlled using **user-IDs/usernames** and passwords. Other authentication techniques involve **biometrics** such as iris scanning, **retinal** scanning and fingerprint recognition.

Changing passwords **regularly/often** means that if someone has managed to find out your password, they can use it only for a short while.

Sensitive data such as credit card numbers are **encrypted** when sent using the internet. Even if the data is intercepted by **hackers** it cannot be understood.

In many countries the misuse of **personal** data is made illegal under a Data **Protection** act.

Fax communication can be made using a **physical** fax which is the traditional method that uses a scanner that scans the page and the data is converted to a series of **sounds** that are sent along a telephone line. A physical fax converts the sounds back to an image at the other end and prints out the fax.

A more up-to-date method is electronic/internet faxing where the fax is sent and received using the internet. The faxes can be read on the **screen/monitor** and printed out only if necessary.

10 MINUTE TEST

1 Router, Hub, Bridge and Switch.

2

	true	false
A firewall can be used to secure the data in a computer connected to the internet.	✔	
An advantage of video-conferencing is the initial cost of the hardware.		✔
A web browser is needed to view web pages.	✔	
A WLAN uses fibre optic cables for communication.		✔
Bluetooth has a greater range compared to WiFi.		✔

3

	true	false
Fingerprint recognition can be used as an authentication technique.	✔	
An advantage of networked computers is that fewer printers are needed.	✔	
It is impossible to use a wireless connection to send data from a computer to a printer.		✔
There is a greater risk from hackers when a computer or network is connected to the internet.	✔	
Viruses do not attack networked computers.		✔

4 A WiFi has a greater range compared to Bluetooth.

Bluetooth is primarily used to connect devices without using cables, while WiFi provides high-speed access to the internet.

B A Bluetooth-enabled device such as a smartphone/laptop/tablet is able to communicate with other Bluetooth devices, such as a wireless headset, mp3 player or printer.

WiFi is used to provide high speed access for a number of computers in the home to the internet.

WiFi can be used to set up a small network without using cables for communication.

5 A Local area network

B Network interface card/NIC

C i In a wired LAN wires/cables are used to provide the communication link between the devices in the network. In a WLAN radio signals are used to link the devices in the network.

ii Fewer cables to buy so cheaper. Easier to connect devices wirelessly as there are no cables to connect.

Fewer trailing wires which can be a safety hazard.

You can work anywhere provided you are in range of the wireless signal.

6

	true	false
A bridge always has more than two ports.		✔
A hub does not manage any of the data traffic through it.	✔	
An intranet uses similar technologies to the internet.	✔	
Switches inspect packets of data so that they are forwarded correctly.	✔	
A firewall is antivirus software.		✔

7 A Advantages

Data can be shared as each computer can access the same pool of data.

Hardware such as printers and scanners can be shared so it is cheaper.

All the computers can share a single internet connection which is cheaper.

Networked versions of software can be purchased which is cheaper than buying individual copies.

Easier to take backups centrally rather than rely on individual users to take them.

B Disadvantages

Danger of hackers using the internet to access the network and causing loss of data.

Need technical knowledge to set up a larger network.

Viruses are more likely to spread over a network.

Chapter 5

Exam preparation

1 Programming – people are needed to write the lists of instructions for the computer hardware to do a useful job.

   Delivery drivers – as more people shop online and get goods delivered to their door, more delivery drivers are needed.

   Website designers – most organisations have a website and people are needed to design and set these up.

   Computer repair/setting up networks/troubleshooting – most people have a computer so people are needed to provide them with user support.

Exam-style questions

1 **A i** Repetitive strain injury.
   ii Using the same muscles in hands/arms for long periods without a break can cause RSI.
   iii Take regular breaks.
      Use an ergonomic mouse/wrist rest/copy holder.

   B Back/neck ache
      Eye strain/headaches

Important things to remember

IT has changed employment in a number of ways. For example, people need to be more **flexible** in the hours they work and few will end up doing the **same** job for the whole of their lives. New IT developments mean that constant **retraining** will be needed to use the new technology. There will be fewer jobs in **factories/manufacturing** as more automation is used for assembling products, welding, paint spraying, packing etc. More people will work from **home** using IT equipment such as video-conferencing for meetings.

There will be reduced employment in areas where manual repetitive tasks are now carried out by **robots**. There will be fewer workers in **shops/stores** as more of us shop online. Job designing and producing CDs/DVDs for films and music will disappear as more of us **download** these.

IT will change working patterns in organisations. There will be **greater/more** availability of part-time work, the opportunity to work **flexible** hours, the opportunity to job **share** and the opportunity to work compressed **hours**.

Microprocessor-controlled devices used in the home include computers, children's **games/toys**, heating systems, alarm systems and intelligent ovens, microwaves and fridges.

Many of these devices save time and mean that people have more **leisure** time. Keeping in touch with family is made easier with mobile phones, email and social **networking** sites. Cheap international calls over the internet can be made using a service called **VOIP**. Many devices such as robot vacuum cleaners, washing machines etc. perform some of the **manual** jobs in the home but this can make you lazy and unhealthy through lack of exercise.

You also do not need to leave your home as **often** as many tasks such as shopping, banking, paying bills, research, entertainment etc. can be completed using the internet.

Staying at home too much has its problems such as lack of **exercise** and lack of social interaction with others.

The use of computers can lead to health problems and the main ones are back and neck ache, repetitive **strain** injury, eye **strain** and headaches. RSI is caused by using a **keyboard** or mouse for long periods without a break. Not sitting upright in your chair can give **back** and neck ache. A dirty screen or screen flicker can give **headaches**.

Back or neck **ache** can be caused by incorrect **posture**. Looking at the screen all day can give you **eye strain**. To prevent back or neck ache you should use an adjustable **chair** which can be adjusted to the correct height.

 **10** *MINUTE TEST*

1 Can lead to laziness, Can lead to unhealthy eating, Manual household skills are lost, Can lead to lack of fitness

2

Sit up straight at all times in your chair.	✔
Make sure there are no trailing wires which could present a tripping hazard.	
Take regular breaks when working at your computer.	✔
Always use a chair where the height can be adjusted.	✔
Make sure that waste paper bins are emptied regularly.	

3

	true	false
Washing machines, microwaves, alarms, air-conditioning and computers all make use of microprocessors.	✔	
You do not need to be in the house when clothes are being washed.	✔	
There is less time for social interactions.		✔
You have to be in the house when food is cooking.		✔
You can get robots that vacuum and mop your floors automatically.	✔	

4 Take regular breaks.

Use an ergonomic keyboard/mouse.

Learn how to type properly – two finger typing has been found to be much worse for RSI.

Use a document holder.

Keep your wrists straight when keying in.

Position the mouse so that it can be used keeping the wrist straight.

Use a wrist rest.

5 You do not need to do a lot of the jobs manually.

You do not need to be present when clothes are being washed.

Robot floor cleaners can vacuum and wash the floors automatically.

You do not need to be present when food is being cooked.

More time is made available to spend with family.

More leisure time to do things you enjoy.

Smart fridges can analyse food constituents so this can lead to a healthier lifestyle.

Fitness machines are available so you do not need to leave the house to go to the gym.

Can lead to unhealthy eating (e.g. microwave meals).

Manual household skills are lost.

You do not get exercise doing household tasks.

Can lead to laziness as lots of tasks can be done for you.

6 See Section 5.1, page 48.

Chapter 6

Exam preparation

1   Robots can work continuously (24/7).

Robots do not need paying although the initial cost of the robots is high.

Robots can work to a greater degree of accuracy compared to humans.

Robots can work in hazardous areas such as the room where car panels are spray painted. It would be dangerous for humans to breathe in the fumes.

Robots take jobs away from humans, although some jobs such as maintaining or programming the robots are created.

Exam-style question

1   A   i   The pre-set value is the ideal value of the temperature for the room as set by the user.

      ii   Processing involved:

- A sensor measures the temperature and inputs the reading into the microprocessor.
- The processor compares the input value with the pre-set value.
- If the temperature value measured by the sensor is less than the pre-set value then the heater is turned on (or stays on if it is already on).
- If the temperature value measured by the sensor is the same or greater than the pre-set value, the heater is turned off.
- The processor sends signals to an output device (i.e. heater) to turn it on or off.
- The process above is continuous.

  B   **Advantages**

Can operate continuously, 24 hours per day and 7 days per week.

You do not need to keep manually adjusting the heating.

The temperature is kept more constant leading to better conditions.

Disadvantages:

Equipment can go wrong leading to poor conditions.

The initial cost of the control equipment.

Important things to remember

There are many different ways of communicating using ICT. For example, ICT can be used to prepare paper-based documents such as newsletters, flyer and posters. You can also communicate using **instant** messaging, phone calls and websites. A technology called **VoIP** allows cheap international phone calls to be made using the **Internet**.

Data handling applications include the processing of survey lists, address lists, club and society records, school reports and school libraries.

Computers can be used for measurement and these systems use **sensors** to input the data automatically. Data can be of two types: **analogue** and digital. Analogue data does not jump from one value to the next and before this can be processed by a computer it needs to be converted to digital data using an **analogue** to digital converter.

Microprocessors are also used in control where sensors are used to **input** data into the computer. The value of the data is compared with a **preset** value to see whether it is lower, the same as, or higher. The processor can then decide which **output** devices to turn on or off.

Computers can be used for the construction of computer **models** which can be used to construct 'what if' scenarios. Computer-controlled **robots** are used for assembling components on production lines and have replaced a lot of repetitive **manual** jobs.

Most schools use a computer system called a school **management** system which performs many routine tasks such as keeping records of student details, attendance and marks for tests. These systems can also be used for preparing **reports**, organising examinations and working out cover for absent teachers.

Booking systems are used by travel, theatre and cinema companies. These booking systems ensure that seats cannot be **double** booked.

Banks use lots of different IT systems. They use a system called **EFT** for transferring funds electronically between banks. Computers also control **ATMs** which are popularly called cash machines. They are also used to process credit/debit card transactions and bank **cheques** using direct data entry using magnetic ink characters.

Computers are used in medicine for the keeping of patient records, pharmacy records and **monitoring** of patients in intensive care departments. **Expert** systems are used by doctors to aid medical diagnoses. These systems consist of four components: an interactive user interface, an **inference** engine, a **rules** base and a knowledge **base**.

Computers are used in libraries to record books and borrowers. Barcodes are used but many libraries now use **RFID** tags as they can be read from a distance and hold more information.

Most large stores use EFTPOS terminals where the customer makes a debit/credit card payment using a chip and **PIN** reader. The validity of the card is checked and the money is transferred electronically from the customer's bank account to the store's bank account.

Recognition systems are used for direct data entry in many different applications such as **optical** mark recognition for marking multiple choice examination papers, optical **character** recognition for recognising car number plates on entry to a car park and **RFID** tags in passports to check if a person should be allowed entry at border control.

To obtain the exact position of a point on the Earth's surface **GPS** is used and when used with a map this system becomes a **satellite navigation** system which many people have in their cars.

 **10 MINUTE TEST**

1 Interactive user interface, Knowledge base, Rules base, Inference engine.

2

Using a camera and OCR software to recognise a car to allow it entry to an airport car park.	✔
Typing in monthly expenses into a computer model.	
Making a low value payment at a shop using a debit card with an RFID chip.	✔
Using OMR to input the responses to a survey.	✔
Keying in the data to create a business card.	

3

	true	false
Expert systems can be used for mineral/oil prospecting.	✔	
Expert systems do not need human experts for their development.		✔
There are five components of an expert system.		✔
A rules base is part of an expert system.	✔	
The user is not asked any questions as all the answers are known.		✔

4 See Section 6.10, page 61.

5 See Section 6.13, page 63-65.

6 A To make sure they are not wasting company time surfing the net.
To check they are not accessing inappropriate sites.

To check they are not performing an illegal activity such as downloading pirated software or music.

To check the emails being sent to customers are appropriate.

B To check what was said in case of a dispute.

To check that the phone calls present the correct image of the company.

To check that lots of private calls are not being made in the company's time.

Chapter 7

Exam preparation

1

Documentation	User	Technical	Both
Hardware requirements.			✔
Software requirements.			✔
How to use the system.	✔		
Limitations of the system.			✔
Frequently asked questions.	✔		
Trouble-shooting guide.	✔		
Test plans.		✔	
Purpose of the system.			✔
Program listings/program code.		✔	
User interface designs.		✔	

Exam-style questions

1 A and B   See Section 7.4, page 76.

2   See Section 7.2, page 74.

Important things to remember

The **systems life cycle** is the series of stages that have to be completed in order to create a new or modified computer system. It consists of **six** stages, the first of which is the **analysis** of the existing or proposed new system. At the end of this stage a document called the **system specification** is produced which outlines the hardware and **software** for the new system.

After the analysis, the **design** stage produces the designs for the system. Data **capture** forms are designed for the input of data, screen **layouts** are produced for the user interface, **validation** routines are designed to prevent invalid data from being entered and details of output designs are produced.

Development and testing is the next stage and in this stage the system is produced and tested. A **test plan** is produced that will include all the data that is used to test the parts of the system. Normal, **abnormal** and extreme data are used to test the system.

The **implementation** stage is the stage where the users change from one system to another. There are four methods of implementation; direct changeover, **parallel** running, **phased** implementation and pilot running.

The next stage is the **documentation** stage where both user and technical documentation are produced.

The sixth and last stage is the **evaluation** stage, where the efficiency of the solution, the ease of use and the appropriateness of the solution are looked at.

10 MINUTE TEST

1

	true	false
Analysis looks at the current system or the requirements of a task.	✔	
The development and testing stage comes after the implementation stage.		✔
Using questionnaires is a method of implementation.		✔
A system specification is produced during the analysis stage.	✔	
Validation routines are designed in the development and testing stage.		✔

2

	true	false
Validation checks will always prevent wrong data from being entered.		✔
A presence check can be used with a field such as gender which must always be entered.	✔	
Range checks are performed on numbers.	✔	
Double entry of data is a method of validation.		✔
Visual checking is a method of verification.	✔	

3 See Section 7.4, page 76.

4

	Normal data	Abnormal data	Extreme data
0		✔	
1			✔
Twenty five		✔	
15.5		✔	
34	✔		
50			✔

5 A Range check

Data type check

B 0 or 40 as extreme data to check the limits of the range check.

30 as normal data to check the range check accepts normal data.

56 as abnormal data to check that the range check will not accept data outside the range.

Twenty five to see if the data type check rejects it as only numbers should be entered.

Chapter 8

Exam preparation

1 A A program/programming code

That can copy/replicate itself

Usually obtained from downloads/email attachments

That can cause damage to or deletion of files

That can cause the cause the computer to run slow by tying up memory

That can cause unexpected computer crashes

B Gaining unauthorised access to a computer system

With the view of viewing/altering the data

With a view to stealing personal information such as banking/card details to commit fraud.

Exam-style questions

1 A See Section 8.2, page 83.
   B See Section 8.2, page 83.

2 A See Section 8.3, page 86.
   B See Section 8.3, page 87.
   C See Section 8.3, page 85.

Important things to remember

Physical safety is about ensuring that you do not come to any harm while working with computer equipment. Computers produce lots of heat and can cause an unhealthy working environment which can be solved by installing **air conditioning**. Using **overloaded** power sockets can lead to **fires** and this can be solved by installing plenty of power sockets in computer rooms. Cables present **tripping** hazards and this safety issue can be solved by sinking or covering cables with carpet. Spilling drinks over computer equipment can cause **electrocution** and to minimise the danger, liquids should not be allowed near computers.

E-safety is about using the internet in a safe and responsible way. There is a dangerous side to the internet so you need to keep yourself **safe**. This means taking precautions such as not agreeing to **meet** an online friend on your own, or giving out **personal** details, and only using websites suggested by parents or teachers.

Hacking is the process of accessing a computer system without permission. Hackers seek to steal and use personal information such as **credit/debit** card and banking details to commit fraud.

Authentication techniques are used to ensure that the user of a network/internet is genuine. **Passwords** known only to the user, digital certificates and biometric methods are used to authenticate a user.

To ensure the security of messages sent using the internet **digital** certificates can be used to ensure that a message sent by someone is definitely from them and not by someone pretending to be them. When goods are paid for on a website, card details are entered using a system called **secure** socket **layer** which encrypts the details so that if they are intercepted by **hackers** the details cannot be understood.

People often try to obtain your bank/card details using the following methods.

Pharming is where malicious programming code is stored on a computer and when the user tries to access a genuine site, the program directs them to a bogus site which attempts to steal their banking details. **Phishing** uses emails pretending to be from a bank, building society, credit card company, etc., and they usually ask you to confirm your banking details which are then used to commit fraud. **Smishing** uses text messaging (SMS) to send fraudulent messages that try to steal your credit card, banking or other personal details.

An online forum is a discussion on the **internet**. **Moderated** forums have a person called a moderator who checks the comments before posting them on the forum. **Un-moderated** forums allow people to post whatever they want on the forum so you can get rude and offensive messages.

Spam is unsolicited email that is sent automatically to multiple recipients. It is a nuisance because it takes time to read and **delete**.

A **virus** is a program that replicates (i.e., copies) itself automatically and can alter or **delete** files. Viruses can be detected and removed using **antivirus** software and to be useful the computer must be **scanned** regularly and the software **updated** regularly.

Many people now store data in the cloud and this means that it is stored on a server somewhere which is regularly **backed** up so you need not worry about taking backups yourself.

(10) MINUTE TEST

1

	true	false
Phishing uses emails to obtain personal information such as passwords and card details.	✔	
Pharming uses malicious programming code which is loaded onto your computer without your knowledge.	✔	
Smishing is a virus that deletes personal data from your computer.		✔
Spam is a type of encryption technique used when sending banking details using the internet.		✔
Encryption scrambles personal data when it is sent using the internet.	✔	

2

	true	false
A virus is a program that copies itself automatically and so can spread to many computers.	✔	
Key logging software is used to help you keep track of your passwords.		✔
Antivirus software can scan your computer for viruses and then help remove them.	✔	
You should never follow a link and then enter your credit card details.	✔	
Antivirus software is never updated.		✔

3 A See Section 8.3, page 85.
   B See Section 8.3, page 86.
   C See Section 8.3, page 86.

4   A   E-safety is concerned with using the internet in a safe and responsible way, such as not giving personal details out online in chat rooms or on social media sites.

Physical safety is about not being harmed by computers or their equipment causing an accident.

B   Electrocution – faulty equipment must be removed immediately and must not be tampered with/do not drink near electrical equipment.

Tripping hazard – cables must be sunk or put under floor covering so that people do not trip over them.

Fire – overloaded electrical sockets are a fire hazard so properly fitted sockets should be installed by an electrician.

Overheating – if some devices have ventilation vents covered they can overheat and possibly catch fire. Ensure that all devices are properly ventilated.

5   A health risk is a risk that is not accidental that develops over time usually through the incorrect use of computer equipment.

A physical safety risk is something that is likely to cause an accident such as a trailing wire that can be tripped over.

6   A   Consists of lots of characters.

Consists of uppercase and lowercase characters.

Consists of punctuation marks and symbols.

Is not your nickname, name of a pet, name of a football team, etc., which can be easily guessed.

B   See Section 8.3, page 84.

Chapter 9

Exam preparation

1   A   The copying of computer software without the copyright owner's permission or the correct licence.

B   It deprives them of income, which is stealing from them.
It will put them off from putting money into the development of new software.

C   It is illegal and you could be prosecuted.
You would be stealing from the software manufacturer.
Copied software is frequently a source of computer viruses.
Some of the money could be used for organised crime.

Exam-style questions

1   A   Films and TV programmes are policed so the internet should be.

There is a lot of undesirable information on the internet such as how to grow drugs, how to make explosives, etc., and this information should be removed.

B   It would be hard because what is legal in one country is illegal in another.

Policing the internet would need agreement from all countries and this would be almost impossible.

The internet is global and it may be hard to define which country's laws should be applied to the content.

Policing the internet would take up too many resources.

2 Copying software illegally is theft as it deprives the copyright owner of income.

The copyright owner will not develop new software if they keep getting it pirated and this affects progress in IT.

The money from software piracy is often used to fund other illegal activities such as drugs and people smuggling.

Important things to remember

When designing and developing an ICT publication or product, you need to consider the intended **audience** who could be adults, teenagers, etc. Different audiences have different **needs** which must be met.

Illegal copying of computer software is called software **piracy**. Copyright **legislation/law** makes it an offence to copy or steal computer software. It also makes it an offence to copy any other **copyrighted** work such as text, images, music, designs of user interfaces, etc. Copying software illegally is no different from stealing as it deprives someone of **money**. In some cases the selling of illegal software,

music and films is used to fund other **illegal** activities such as selling drugs and people trafficking. You should not download illegally copied software/games as they are often used to distribute **viruses** which can infect your computer.

One method software producers use to prevent illegal copying of software is by the use of a **dongle** which can be either hardware or software. Some software producers **encrypt** the execution code of the software so that a key is needed to unlock the code and allow the software to run.

 **(10) MINUTE TEST**

1

	true	false
Copyright laws only cover computer software.		✔
It is always illegal to copy computer software.		✔
Copying software illegally is called software piracy.	✔	
Software licences usually allow software to be copied under certain circumstances (e.g. backup copies).	✔	
Copying software onto more than one computer is always illegal.		✔

2

	true	false
Encryption of the execution code means that a key is needed to run the software.	✔	
A piece of hardware that attaches to the USB port to allow secured software to run is called a dangle.		✔
An activation key is sometimes used which is long code that needs to be typed in when on the software manufacturer's website.	✔	
Guards are hardware or software that monitor whether programming code is altered in some way.	✔	

3 See table in Section 9.1, page 93.

4 A To protect people who have invested time and money into developing software, music, etc., against having their work stolen.

To ensure that people will develop new software/material without the fear that their work will be copied.

B See Section 9.2, page 93.

Chapter 10

Exam preparation

1 Check how up-to-date the information is/check when the web page was last updated.

Only use sites produced by organisations you have heard of (e.g., newspapers, BBC, etc.).

Use several sites to get the information and check that the sites are giving similar information.

Follow the links to see if they work. Many bogus sites have links that do not work.

Check if the site has spelling mistakes/bad grammar and if so it will not have been checked properly so don't use the information.

Exam-style questions

1 Benefits

Easy to keep in immediate contact with friends/make new friends.

Easy to communicate with more than one friend/to communicate with people overseas.

Can search for people who you've lost touch with.

Easy to arrange meetings/visits to cinema/theatre.

Can share photographs/videos/images/opinions/views.

Drawbacks

Sites can be used to spread gossip/rumours/lies.

Can be used for online bullying.

Invades your privacy.

Personal data can be given out which can put you in danger.

2 Benefits

The information is often dated so you can check if it is up-to-date.

It is faster to do searches rather than look through books in a library.

The internet has a huge amount of information so it is likely you will find the required information.

Search engines are very fast at finding results.

Drawbacks

It can take a long time to find the relevant information.

The information obtained may not have been recently updated.

The material may be inaccurate.

You could access a biased/bogus website.

There is a tendency to plagiarise information as it is so easy to copy and paste.

You need to be proficient at constructing searches, which takes time.

Important things to remember

An **email** is an electronic message sent from one communication device (such as a smartphone, tablet or computer) to another using the internet. **Groups** are lists of people who may need to be sent the same email. There are a number of **constraints** which affect the way email is used. For example in some countries emails are **monitored/censored** which means other people can read their contents and then decide whether or not it should be sent to the intended recipient. You should use **appropriate** language in your emails and not infringe **copyright**. Many employers have **guidelines** covering what an employee can and cannot do using email. Emails are **password** protected in order to prevent unauthorised access. When writing emails you must learn to abide by certain rules called **netiquette** and these include such things as not using all capitals as this is considered to be 'shouting' and making sure that emails are short and to the point.

Email sent in bulk to lots of people is called **spam** which clogs up your inbox and slows down the network. Spam **filters** are able to recognise some email as being spam and these emails are put into a separate folder for deletion.

A web **browser** is an application installed on your computer that provides you a graphical user interface for accessing the internet.

A search engine is an application typically installed on a server at a company's data centre that you access via your **web browser**.

Ways of transferring data using the internet are called **protocols** and these are a set of **rules** governing the format of the data and the signals to start, control, and end the transfer of data.

HTTP (HyperText **Transfer** Protocol) is a protocol that defines the process of identifying, requesting, and transferring multimedia web pages over the internet. HTTPS (HyperText Transfer Protocol secure variant) – is like HTTP except it uses **encrypted** connections to hide passwords, bank information, and other sensitive material from the open network to prevent hackers accessing and using the data.

A uniform resource **locator** (URL) is another name for a web address, and the feature of the internet that allows a user to jump to a new web page or document is called a **hyperlink**.

The common protocol for moving files using the internet is called **file transfer protocol** or FTP for short.

A **blog/web log** is an online diary of events and many celebrities have them to let their fans know what they have been doing. A **wiki** is a web page that can be viewed and modified by anyone who has web **browser** software. This means can add your own comments which does cause problems as people can post **offensive** messages.

Social **network/networking** sites help keep people in touch with each other and allows you to search for and find friends you have lost touch with.

10 MINUTE TEST

1

	true	false
Email groups save time if you need to send the same email to several people.	✔	
Spam email is email from people you already know.		✔
Spam is a nuisance as it takes time to delete.	✔	
Typing in all capital letters is a breach of netiquette.	✔	
Copyright laws do not apply to the text in emails.		✔

2

	true	false
A web browser is application software used to provide a graphical user interface for accessing web pages on the internet.	✔	
A search engine is system software.		✔
A URL is a type of web browser.		✔
An ISP is a protocol used for transferring files using the internet.		✔
FTP is a protocol for the movement of files across the internet.	✔	

3 Blog
A blog usually has just one author.
Entries are usually in reverse chronological order.
Usually personal.
Readers can add comments but are we not able to edit the blog.
Uses external links.

Wiki
Wikis usually have many authors.
The structure is determined by the content and users.
Usually objective.
Contributors are able to edit entries.
Both internal and external links are used.

4 A Material is normally up-to-date.
It is quicker to find relevant information.
You can retrieve the information using any device with internet access.
You do not have to leave the house to get the information.
Easy to make a copy of the information.

B It can take time to search for relevant information.
Sometimes there are too many hits and it takes time looking at each.
You may encounter inappropriate material.
The information may not be reliable.

C Check the date that the site was last updated.
Only use sites produced by organisations you have heard of.
Use several sites to get the information and check that the sites are giving similar information.
Follow the links to see if they work as bogus sites have links which don't work.

5 A A private network that uses the same technology as the internet for the sending of messages/data around a network.

B Information about the school such as school rules, timetables, past exam results, lists of teachers and their contact details, subject-specific pages, exam timetables, revision material, etc.

C Authentication uses a username and a password to prevent unauthorised access.

Exam Guidance and Practice 3

Paper 1 Theory

1. **A** hard disk
   B RFID tag
   C Memory card
   D Magnetic tape

2. One mark for each correctly placed tick.

	true	false
Antivirus programs are examples of hardware.		✔
A keyboard is an example of an external hardware device.	✔	
Apps or applets are examples of software.	✔	
Video cards are external hardware devices.		✔
Linkers are part of the systems software.	✔	

3. One mark each for the following circled devices.
   magnetic stripe reader
   chip and PIN reader
   barcode reader

4. One mark for each correctly placed tick.

	internet	world wide web
Is a means of accessing information		✔
Consists of computer hardware	✔	
Is a huge network of networks	✔	
Uses http and web browsers to access information		✔

5. **A** One mark for the name of the input method and one mark for a description of how the system is used to mark attendance.

   Biometric method (retinal scanning/recognition, iris scanning/recognition, fingerprint scanning/recognition, face recognition, etc.). Students are recognised by the scanner and their attendance details are recorded.

   Magnetic stripe/swipe cards – each pupil is given a plastic card containing a magnetic stripe which contains identification details which are read by the reader.

   Laptops/tablets networked using WiFi – here the teachers are given laptops/tablets to record pupil attendance on and the details are sent wirelessly to update the school's administration computers.

   B One mark for each explanation of advantage × 2. Explanations include:

   Takes the burden of recording attendance away from the teachers

   Makes the pupils more adult by making them responsible for recording their attendance

Attendance statistics are available immediately so parents can be notified if their children are not present

Harder for pupils to get marked in and then go home

Safer as in an emergency such as a fire the teachers know exactly who is on the premises.

6 **A** One mark each for four features of a relational database such as:

Database that does not store all the data in a single table

They use several tables

Tables are linked together (or mention of relationships)

Data in one table can be combined with data in any of the other tables

Note they must be features and not advantages.

B One mark each for three distinctly different advantages that must be relevant to this application.

Full customer details do not need to be entered when a customer who has rented before, rents again.

If a mailshot needs to go out to customers, the manager will not need to go through all the orders extracting names and addresses as you can use the Customer table.

An update is easier to make as the manager will only need to alter the data the once in one of the tables.

The data is stored more efficiently so it will be faster to do searches and sorts.

There will be fewer data errors since the data is only entered once, which means the manager can rely on the information produced.

7 **A** One mark for each of the following points to a maximum of two marks.

Allows a user to communicate with the computer

The way the computer interacts with the user

It allows the user to make selections

It provides a dialogue between the computer and the user

B One mark for one of the following:

Mouse

Touch pad

Trackerball

Touch screen

Etc.

C Any four from the following (one mark each):

Windows

Icons

Menus/Pull-down menus

Pointers

Online help/Office assistants

D i One mark for one of the following:

Menu driven interface

Command line interface

Voice driven interface

ii One mark each for two benefits such as:

Standard look and feel

Interfaces are similar so they are easier to learn and skills can be transferred

More intuitive (users can usually figure out what they have to do)

Use of icons with pictures makes it easy for users to work out what each button does

8 A Any three advantages (2 marks each) such as:

Email is cheaper than a letter. No stamp, envelope or paper is needed. There is also a time saving so this makes email cheaper. Even if the email is sent across the world, it will not cost any more than a local email.

Quick to write. They are informal, meaning that people do not spend time on the layout and the odd spelling mistake is acceptable.

Ideal if there is a time difference. The reader can check email when they are ready.

Inexpensive and easy to send the same email message to lots of different people.

You can attach a copy of the sender's email with your reply, so this saves them having to search for the original message.

You do not have to go out to a post box, so it saves time.

You do not have to waste time shopping for stamps, envelopes and paper.

Fast. It takes seconds to send and receive email. If the person at the other end checks their email regularly, then a reply can be sent very quickly.

B Two facilities (2 marks each) such as:

Groups/distribution lists – allowing you to send the same email to a group of people without having to select individual email addresses.

File attachments – being able to attach files to an email so others can download the work onto their own computers and can comment on it.

9 A One mark for each part

i Data that should pass the validation check and be accepted for processing.

ii Data that is unacceptable and that should be rejected by the validation check.

iii Data on the borderline of what the system will accept.

B One mark for each item of extreme data 0 and 50.

10 A One mark each for:

A cabled LAN uses cables to transmit the data signals

A WLAN uses radio signals/wireless technology to transmit the data signals.

B One mark for each advantage of a WLAN to a maximum of two marks.

There are fewer cables to cause a tripping hazard.

Cheaper as fewer cables are required.

Users can work anywhere in range of the wireless signal.

It is easy to connect new computers and devices such as printers to the network.

One mark for each disadvantage of a WLAN to a maximum of two marks.

There is a limited range to the wireless signals.

The network is not as secure from hackers.

The data is transmitted more slowly compared to a wired LAN.

Physical obstacles such as walls, metal filing cabinets can limit the range of the wireless signal.

C One mark for each method.

Using usernames and passwords

Using a biometric method such as retinal scanning/fingerprint scanning/iris scanning

11 One mark for each correct statement.

PENDOWN

FORWARD 30

PENUP

FORWARD 20

PENDOWN

FORWARD 20

RIGHT 90

FORWARD 40

LEFT 90

FORWARD 20

LEFT 90

REPEAT 4

FORWARD 30

RIGHT 90

END REPEAT

12 A One mark for each item of personal information (not contact details)

Medical details

Social worker details

Qualifications

Religious beliefs

etc.

B One mark for each of the following:

The right to see the information held and have it corrected or deleted if it is wrong.

The right to compensation if they have suffered harm because the information held has been held illegally.

One mark for each point/example to a maximum of four marks.

Their details could be mixed up with someone else

It could affect them in getting a job

It could affect them getting credit

It could stop them getting the right medical treatment if they were ill

13 A One mark for each point to a maximum of four marks.

Encryption is the scrambling of data (1) using an encryption key (1) before it is stored or transmitted over a network (1) to prevent hackers from understanding the data should it be intercepted (1). The receiver uses a decryption key to unscramble the data (1).

B One mark for each benefit or drawback to a maximum of four marks.

Benefits

Protects personal data from being understood should it be hacked into.

Enables secure communication to be made between two computers.

Only the person with the decryption key can decipher/unscramble and understand the data.

Drawbacks

Data can still be deleted from the system.

Criminals can use encryption to send private messages which the security forces cannot understand.

14 One mark for each advantage/disadvantage up to a maximum of five marks.

Advantages

Can operate continuously, 24 hours per day and 7 days per week

Less expensive to run as you don't have to pay wages.

Can easily change the task the robot does by re-programming it.

More accurate than humans.

Robots can work in inhospitable conditions such as where there are paint fumes when panels are being sprayed.

Disadvantages

Robots take jobs away from humans although some jobs such as maintaining or programming the robots are created.

Deskilling can occur if certain jobs are always carried out by robots.

One mark for a conclusion (either for or against the introduction of robots).

For example.

Robots are here to stay as we need to get them to do the more mundane jobs leaving the humans to do the more interesting and more creative jobs or jobs where robots cannot be used.

15 A One mark for each of the following:

A primary key is a field in a database that is unique to a particular record (i.e. row in a table).

Vehicle_ID should be chosen as it is unique to a particular vehicle.

B i One mark for Air_conditioning

ii There are only two possibilities (i.e. Y or N).

C i One mark for Number_of_doors

ii Only numbers can be entered.

16 One mark for each of the following to a maximum of five marks.

Experts are interviewed.

Data is collected from experts.

Knowledge base is designed and created.

Rules base is designed and created.

Input and output format/screens are designed and made.

Expert system is checked by using known results.

17 One mark for each of the following to a maximum of eight marks.

Advantages

Less stress as employees do not have to experience delays at airports, accidents, road works, etc.

Improved family life, as less time spent away from home staying in hotels.

Saves travelling time.

Saves money as business does not have to spend money on travelling expenses, hotel rooms, meals, etc.

Improved productivity of employees, as they are not wasting time travelling.

Meetings can be called at very short notice without too much planning.

More environmentally friendly as there are fewer people travelling to meetings. This cuts down on carbon dioxide emissions.

Fewer car journeys means fewer traffic jams and hence less stress and pollution.

Disadvantages

The initial cost of the equipment, as specialist video-conferencing equipment is expensive.

Poor image and sound quality.

People can feel very self-conscious when using video-conferencing and not communicate effectively.

Although documents and diagrams in digital form can be passed around, an actual product or component cannot be passed around.

Lack of face-to-face contact may mean a discussion may not be as effective.

If the delegates are in distant locations, the picture can be out of synchronisation with the speech, which can be distracting.

18 One mark for each point to a maximum of six marks.

Desktops are far too heavy to be used in different places whereas the other devices can be.

The keyboard on a desktop is full size which makes it the easiest to use.

Tablets and smartphones use mainly on-screen keyboards which are not as easy to use as physical keyboards.

Tablets and smartphones can be used whilst walking where desktops and laptops cannot.

The smartphone screen is small compared to the others which makes text hard to see all at once.

Smartphones tend to use scaled down versions of the websites that do not have all the features of the full-sized version.

Desktop computers usually have the fastest internet access as they are most likely to use a cable to transfer the data.

Laptops, tablets and smartphones are more likely to be used wirelessly where the internet is not as fast compared to using a cabled data connection.

Lack of a signal (either WiFi or phone) may prevent the internet being accessed by phones or tablets and possibly laptops.

A cabled internet connection to a desktop is likely to be more reliable than wireless connections to the other devices.

You are most likely to have a smartphone with you compared to the other devices, which means internet access is available subject to there being a signal.

You can access the internet from more places using a mobile phone.

Glossary

3D printer printer that can print in three-dimensions by repeatedly building up layers of material.

Abnormal data data that is unacceptable and that should be rejected by a validation check; for example, entering text into a numeric field or inputting data which is outside the range specified.

Absolute reference a reference to a cell used in a formula where, when the formula is copied to a new address, the cell address does not change.

Address book the names and email addresses of all the people to whom you are likely to send email, stored as a file.

Alphanumeric data sometimes called text and it includes letters, digits and punctuation marks.

Analogue a continuously changing quantity that needs to be converted to digital values before it can be processed by a computer.

Analogue-to-digital converter (ADC) a device that changes continuously changing quantities (such as temperature) into digital quantities.

ANPR (automatic number plate recognition) a method using OCR on images obtained from video cameras to read car registration plates.

Antispyware software used to detect and remove spyware which may have been put on your computer without your knowledge or permission.

Antivirus software software that is used to detect and destroy computer viruses.

Applet a program designed to be executed from within another application. Unlike an application, applets cannot be executed directly from the operating system.

Applications software software designed to do a particular job such as word-processing or database software.

Artificial intelligence (AI) creating computer programs or computer systems that behave in a similar way to the human brain by learning from experience, etc.

Aspect ratio the ratio of the width of an image to its height.

ATM (automatic teller machine) another name for a cashpoint/cash dispenser.

Attachment a file which is attached to an email which the recipient can open and view the contents provided they have suitable software to open the file.

Audio-conferencing conducting a meeting held by people in different places using devices that allow voice to be sent and received.

Backing storage storage which is not classed as ROM or RAM. It is used to hold programs and data. Backing storage devices include magnetic hard drives, optical drives (CD or DVD), flash/pen drives, etc.

Backup keeping copies of software and data so that they can be recovered should there be corruption or loss of some or all of the ICT system.

Backup file copy of a file which is used in the event of the original file being corrupted (damaged) or lost.

Bandwidth a measure of the amount of data that can be transferred per second over the internet or other network.

Barcode a series of lines of differing thickness which are used to represent a number which is usually written below the barcode. Can be read by a scanner to input the number accurately.

Batch processing type of processing where all the inputs needed are collected over a period of time and then batched together, inputted and processed in one go. For example, questionnaires from a survey are collected over a few weeks and then batched together and processed in one go.

bcc (blind carbon copy) this is useful when you want to send an email to one person and others but you do not want the others to see each other's email addresses.

Biometric a unique property of the human body such as fingerprints or retinal patterns which can be used to identify a person and allow them access to a computer system.

BIOS (basic input/output system) stored in ROM and holds instructions used to 'boot' (i.e. start up) the computer when first switched on.

Bit a binary digit: 0 or 1.

Blog a website that allows comments to be posted; usually in reverse chronological order.

Blogger a person who maintains a blog.

Bluetooth a method used to wirelessly transfer data over short distances from fixed and mobile devices. The range of Bluetooth depends on the power of the signal and can typically be from 5m to 100m.

Blu-ray optical disk that has a much higher storage capacity than a DVD. Blu-ray disks have capacities of 25 Gb, 50 Gb, and 100 Gb. These high capacity Blu-ray disks are used to store high definition video. They are used for storing films/movies, with a 25 Gb Blu-ray disk being able to store 2 hours of HDTV or 13 hours of standard definition TV. It is possible to play back video on a Blu-ray disk while simultaneously recording HD video.

Bookmark storage area where the URL (i.e. the web address) of a website can be stored so that it can be accessed later using a link.

Boolean data data that can exist in only two states; for example True or False.

Bridge a hardware device used to connect two local area networks to each other. The purpose of a bridge is to decide whether a message needs to be transferred between the two networks or just confined to one of them. This reduces network traffic.

Browser (also called web browser) software program you use to access the internet. Microsoft's Internet Explorer is an example of a web browser.

Bullet point a block or paragraph of text that has a symbol placed in front to make the section of text stand out.

CAD (computer-aided design) software software used to produce technical drawings, plans, designs, maps, etc.

cc (carbon copy) is used when you want to send an email to one person but you also want others to see the email you are sending. To do this you enter the email address of the main person you are sending it to and in the box marked cc you enter all the email addresses, separated by commas, of all the people you wish to receive a copy.

CD R (CD recordable) optical storage where data is stored as an optical pattern. The user can record their data onto the disk once only.

CD ROM (CD read-only memory) optical storage where data is stored as an optical pattern. Once data has been written onto CD ROM it cannot be erased. It is mainly used for the distribution of software.

CD RW (CD rewritable) optical storage that allows data to be stored on the disk over and over again, just like a hard disk. This is needed if the data stored on the disk needs to be updated. You can treat a CD RW like a hard drive but the transfer rate is less and the time taken to locate a file is greater. The media is not as robust as a hard drive.

Cell an area on a spreadsheet produced by the intersection of a column and a row, in which data can be placed.

Changeover the process by which an older ICT system is replaced with a newer one.

Character any symbol (letter, number, punctuation mark, etc.) that you can type from the keyboard.

Check digit a decimal number (or alphanumeric character) added to a number for the purpose of detecting the sorts of errors humans normally make on data entry.

Chip and PIN Chip readers are the devices into which you place a credit/debit card to read the data which is encrypted in the chip on the card. The PIN pad is the small numeric keypad where the personal identification number (PIN) is entered and the holder can be verified as the true owner of the card.

CLI (command line interface) type of user interface where a user has to type in instructions in a certain format to accomplish a task.

Clipboard temporary storage area used for copying or cutting data to, and then pasting it somewhere else.

Cloud computing internet-based computing where programs and data are stored on the internet rather than on the user's own computer.

Command line interface (CLI) type of user interface where a user has to type in instructions in a certain format to accomplish a task.

Compression storing data in a format that requires less space. A compressed file takes less time to be transferred across a network.

Computer Misuse Act a law which makes illegal a number of activities such as deliberately planting viruses, hacking, using ICT equipment for fraud, etc.

Content the actual text, images, etc.

Control system system used to control a process automatically by making use of data from sensors as the input to the system.

Copyright, Designs and Patents Act a law making it a criminal offence to copy or steal software or use the software in a way that is not allowed according to the software licence.

CPU (central processing unit) the computer's brain. It interprets and executes the commands given to it by the hardware and software.

Cropping only using part of an image.

CSS (cascading style sheet) file used to format the contents of a web page. The file contains properties on how to display HTML elements. HTML is a special code used for making web pages. For example, a user can define the size, colour, font, line spacing, indentation, borders, and location of HTML elements. CSS files are used to create a similar look and feel across all the web pages in a website.

CSV comma separated variables. A way of holding data in a file so that it can be transferred into databases or spreadsheets.

Data raw facts and figures, e.g. readings from sensors, survey facts, etc.

Data capture term for the various methods by which data can be entered into the computer so that it can be processed.

Data logger a device which collects readings from one or more sensors. The time interval between each reading can be varied (called the logging rate) and the total time over which the data is logged (called the logging period) can also be varied.

Data logging the process of using an ICT system to collect data from sensors at a certain rate over a certain period of time. Remote weather stations use data logging.

Data Protection Act an act that restricts the way personal information is stored and processed on a computer.

Data redundancy where the same data is stored more than once in a table or where the same data is stored in more than one table.

Data type check validation check to ensure the data being entered is the same type as the data type specified for the field.

Database a collection of data stored in a computer which can be accessed in a variety of different ways.

Device driver a short, specially written program that understands the operation of the device it controls/operates. For example, driver software can operate/control a printer or scanner. Driver software is needed so as to allow the systems or applications software to control the device properly.

Digital camera a camera that takes a picture and stores it digitally so that it can be transferred to and processed by a computer or other device.

Digital certificate An electronic passport that allows a person, computer or organisation to

exchange information securely using the internet. The digital certificate provides identifying information and is issued by a trusted body.

Digital-to-analogue converter (DAC) a device that changes digital quantities into analogue ones.

Direct/random access data is accessed immediately from the storage media. This is the method used with storage media such as magnetic hard disks and optical media such as CD and DVD.

Dot matrix printer a printer which uses numerous tiny dots to make up each printed character. It works by hitting tiny pins against an inked ribbon to make the dots on the page, making this type of printer rather noisy.

Double entry of data entering the details into an ICT system twice; only if the two sets of data are identical will they be accepted for processing. It is a method of verification. This method is often used when you set up a new password.

Download to copy files from a distant computer to the one you are working on.

Drag and drop allows you to select objects (icons, folders, files etc.) and drag them so that you can perform certain operations on them such as drag to the recycle bin to discard, add a file to a folder, copy files to a folder and so on.

DVD R (DVD recordable) a type of optical storage. DVD R allows data to be stored on a DVD only once.

DVD ROM (digital versatile disk read-only memory) DVD ROM is optical storage and offers much higher storage capacity compared to CD. It is used for the distribution of movies where you can only

read the data off the disk. A DVD ROM drive can also be used for the reading of data off a CD. DVD is mainly used for the distribution of films and multimedia encyclopaedias.

EFTPOS (Electronic funds transfer at point of sale) where electronic funds transfer takes place at a point of sale terminal. This means that money is transferred from the bank or credit card company to the store when you pay for goods at a store.

Encryption the process of coding files before they are sent over a network to protect them from hackers. Also the process of coding files stored on a computer/storage device so that if the computer/storage device is stolen, the files cannot be read. Only the person who has a special key can see the information in its original form.

EPOS (Electronic point of sale) a computerised till which can be used for stock control.

Ergonomics an applied science concerned with designing and arranging things people use so that the people and things interact most efficiently and safely.

E-safety using the internet in a safe and responsible way.

Evaluation the act of reviewing what has been achieved, how it was achieved and how well the solution works.

Expert system an ICT system that mimics the decision-making ability of a human expert.

External hardware devices those hardware devices situated outside the computer casing.

Extreme data is data on the borderline of what the system will accept. For example, if a range check specifies that a number from 16 to 21 inclusive is entered, the extreme data would be 16 and 21.

Favourites storage area where the URL (the web address) of a website can be stored so that it can be accessed later using a link.

Fax a machine capable of sending and receiving text and pictures along telephone lines.

Field a space in an information handling system/database used for inputting data. For instance, you could have fields for surname, date of birth, etc.

File a collection of related data.

File attachment (sometimes called an attachment) a file that is attached to an email and can be sent to another person or a group of people.

File compression using special software to reduce file size before sending them over the internet or to reduce their size so that they take up less space on the storage media.

File Transfer Protocol (FTP) a common protocol for the movement of files across the internet. Users can access a server that contains the file they want and then download it to their computer using FTP. Alternatively, they can upload a file to the server from their computer using FTP.

Firewall a piece of software, hardware or both that is able to protect a network from hackers.

Flash/pen drives portable storage media which offer cheap and large storage capacities and are ideal media for photographs, music and other data files. They consist of printed circuit boards enclosed in a plastic case.

Flat file method used for storage of data in a database where all the data is held in a single table.

Font a set of letters and characters in a particular design.

Footer text placed at the bottom of a document.

Format checks checks performed on codes to make sure that they conform to the correct combinations of characters.

Generic file formats file formats that are able to be used by different software no matter who the manufacturer of the software is.

GIF (Graphics Interchange Format) file type used for images. Images in this format are reduced to a maximum of 256 colours. Images in this format are compressed so this means that they load quickly. Used for simple line diagrams or clip art.

GIGO abbreviation for garbage in garbage out. It means that if you put rubbish into the computer then you get rubbish out.

GIS (Geographic information system) an ICT system that is used to capture, manage, analyse and display geographically referenced information.

GPS (Global Positioning System) system which uses the signals from several satellites to obtain the exact position of any object (e.g. aircraft, ship, car, etc.) on the Earth's surface. Many cars are equipped with satellite navigation systems which use GPS so that the driver can locate their position on a map on a small screen inside the car.

Graph plotter an output device which draws by moving a pen. Useful for scale drawings and is used mainly with CAD packages.

Geographic information system (GIS) an ICT system that is used to capture, manage, analyse and display geographically referenced information.

Graphics tablet an input device which consists of shapes and commands on a tablet which can be selected by the user by touching. The use of a graphics

tablet means that more space is left on the screen for a plan or diagram.

GUI (graphical user interface) interface that allows users to communicate with the computer using windows, icons, menus and pointers.

Hackers people who break into a computer/computer network illegally.

Hacking process of trying to break into a secure computer system.

Hard copy printed output from a computer which may be taken away and studied.

Hardware the physical components of a computer system.

Header text placed at the top of a document.

Hot spot an image or piece of text used as a link. When you click on the image or text, you are taken to another part of the same page, a different page or a different site, or it may open a new file or a new window.

htm a popular file format used for storing web pages.

HTTP (HyperText Transfer Protocol) a protocol that defines the process of identifying, requesting and transferring multimedia web pages over the internet.

HTTPS (HyperText Transfer Protocol secure variant) a protocol that defines the process of identifying, requesting and transferring multimedia web pages over the internet, except unlike HTTP it uses encrypted connections to hide passwords, bank information and other sensitive material from the open network.

Hub a hub contains multiple ports (i.e. connection points). When a packet of data arrives at one port, it is copied to the other ports so that all network devices of the LAN can see all packets. Every device on the network will receive the packet of data which it will inspect to see if it is relevant or not.

Hyperlink a feature of a website that allows a user to jump to another web page, to jump to part of the same web page or to send an email message.

Hypertext Mark-Up Language (HTML) a code used to create documents on the world wide web. You use it to specify the structure and layout of a web document.

Identity theft using someone's banking/credit card/personal details in order to commit fraud.

Inference engine one of four parts of an expert system. It uses the input data along with the rules in the rules base and the knowledge in the knowledge base to arrive at conclusions/decisions/answers which are output using the user interface.

Inkjet printer printer that works by spraying ink through nozzles onto the paper.

Input device the hardware device used to feed the input data into an ICT system such as a keyboard or a scanner.

Instant messaging (IM) a method of two people using real-time text to conduct a conversation using the internet.

Integer a whole number which can be positive, negative or zero.

Interactive where there is a constant dialogue between the user and the computer.

Internal hardware devices those hardware devices situated inside the computer casing.

Internal memory memory inside the computer casing (e.g. ROM, RAM and internal hard disk).

Internet a huge group of networks joined together. The largest network in the world.

Internet service provider (ISP) a company that provides an internet connection.

Intranet a private network

used within an organisation that makes uses of internet technology (e.g. web pages and web browsers) used for sharing internal information.

IP (Internet Protocol) address a number which uniquely identifies the physical computer linked to the internet.

Joystick input device used instead of the cursor keys or mouse as a way of producing movement on the screen.

JPEG a file format used for still images which uses millions of colours and compression, which makes it an ideal file format for photographic images on web pages.

K Kilobyte or 1024 bytes. Often abbreviated as KB. A measure of the storage capacity of disks and memory.

Key field this is a field that is unique for a particular record in a database.

Key logging the process of someone recording/monitoring the keys you press when you are using your computer using a key logger which can either be hardware or software. As it can record keystrokes, someone might secretly record your passwords and banking details.

Knowledge base one of four parts of an expert system. A huge organised set of knowledge about a particular subject. It contains facts and also judgemental knowledge, which gives it the ability to make a good guess, like a human expert.

LAN (local area network) a network of computers on one site.

Landscape page orientation where the width is greater than the height.

Laser printer printer which uses

a laser beam to form characters on the paper.

LCD (liquid crystal display) technology used with thin flat screens.

Length check validation check to make sure that the data being entered has the correct number of characters in it.

Light pen input device used to draw directly on a computer screen or used to make selections on the screen.

Linkers programs that are usually part of the compiler which take care of the linking between the code the programmer writes and other resources and libraries that make up the whole program file that can be executed (run).

Login accessing an ICT system usually by entering a user-ID/username and/or a password.

Magnetic stripe stripe on a plastic card where data is encoded in a magnetic pattern on the stripe and can be read by swiping the card using a magnetic stripe reader.

Magnetic stripe reader hardware device that reads the data contained in magnetic stripes such as those on the back of debit/credit cards.

Mail merge combining a list of names and addresses with a standard letter so that a series of letters is produced with each letter being addressed to a different person.

Main internal memory memory which is either ROM (read only memory) or RAM (random access memory).

Master slides (also called slide masters) used to help ensure consistency from slide to slide in a presentation. They are also used to place objects and set styles on each slide. Using master slides you can format titles, backgrounds, colour schemes, dates, slide numbers, etc.

Megabyte a unit of file or memory size that is 1024 kilobytes.

Megapixel one million pixels (i.e. dots of light).

Memory cards thin cards you see in digital cameras used to store photographs and can be used for other data.

Memory stick/flash drive/pen drive solid state memory used for backup and is usually connected to the computer using a USB port.

MICR (magnetic ink character recognition) system used for cheque clearing which is able to read data printed onto cheques in magnetic ink.

Microprocessor the brain of the computer consisting of millions of tiny circuits on a silicon chip. It processes the input data to produce information.

MIDI (musical instrument digital interface) enables a computer and musical instrument to communicate with each other.

Monitor another name for a VDU or computer screen.

Motherboard the main printed circuit board in a computer that connects the central processing unit, memory and connectors to the external hardware devices such as keyboard, screen, mouse, etc.

MP3 music file format that uses compression to reduce the file size considerably, which is why the MP3 file format is popular with portable music players such as iPods and mobile phones.

Multimedia making use of many media such as text, image, sound, animation and video.

Multimedia projector output device used to project the screen display from a computer onto a much larger screen that can be viewed by a large audience.

Network group of ICT devices (computers, printers, scanners etc.) which are able to communicate with each other.

Network interface card (NIC) circuit board which connects to the motherboard of the computer. It prepares the data ready for sending over a network. It includes connectors that allow connection to network cables.

Networking software systems software which allows computers connected together to function as a network.

Normal data data that is acceptable for processing and will pass the validation checks.

OCR (optical character recognition) a combination of software and a scanner which is able to read characters into the computer.

OMR (optical mark reader/ recognition) reader that detects marks on a piece of paper. Shaded areas are detected and the computer can read the information contained in them.

Online processing the system is automatically updated when a change (called a transaction) is made. This means that the system always contains up-to-date information. Online processing is used with booking systems to ensure seats are not double booked.

Online shopping shopping over the internet as opposed to using traditional methods such as buying goods or services from shops or trading using the telephone.

Operating system software that controls the hardware of a computer and is used to run the applications software. Operating systems control the handling of input, output, interrupts, etc.

Optical character recognition (OCR) input method using a scanner as the input device along with special software which looks at the shape of each character so that it can be recognised separately.

Optical disk a plastic disk used for removable storage. Includes CD and DVD.

Optical mark recognition (OMR) the process of reading marks (usually shaded boxes) made on a specially prepared document. The marks are read using an optical mark reader.

Output the results from processing data.

Password a series of characters chosen by the user that are used to check the identity of the user when they require access to an ICT system.

pdf (portable document format) used with a particular piece of applications software for viewing documents. This file format is used by the software Adobe Acrobat. This file format is popular because the software used to view the files is widely available and free.

Personal data data about a living identifiable person which is specific to that person.

Pharming malicious programming code is stored on a computer. Any users who try to access a website which has been stored on the computer will be re-directed automatically by the malicious code to a bogus website and not the website they wanted. The fake or bogus website is often used to obtain passwords or banking details so that these can be used fraudulently.

Phishing fraudulently trying to get people to reveal usernames, passwords, credit card details, account numbers, etc., by pretending to be from a bank, building society, or credit card company, etc. Emails are sent asking recipients to reveal their details.

PIN (personal identification number) secret number that

needs to be keyed in to gain access to an ATM or to pay for goods/services using a credit/debit card.

Piracy the process of illegally copying software.

Pixel a single point in a graphics element or the smallest dot of light that can appear on a computer screen.

Plotter a device which draws by moving a pen. Useful for printing scale drawings, designs and maps.

Podcast a digital radio broadcast created using a microphone, computer and audio editing software. The resulting file is saved in MP3 format and then uploaded onto an internet server. It can then be downloaded using a facility called RSS onto an MP3 player for storing and then listening.

Point a length which is 1/72 inch. Font size is measured in points. For example, font size of 12 pts means 12/72=1/6 inch which is the height the characters will be.

Portrait page orientation where the height is greater than the width.

Presence checks validation checks used to ensure that data has been entered into a field.

Print preview feature that comes with most software used to produce documents. It allows users to view the page or pages of a document to see exactly how they will be printed. If necessary, the documents can be corrected. Print preview saves paper and ink.

Process any operation that transfers data into information.

Processing performing something on the input data such as performing calculations, making decisions or arranging the data into a meaningful order.

Processor often called the CPU and is the brain of the computer consisting of millions of tiny circuits on a silicon chip. It processes the input data to produce information.

Program the set of step-by-step instructions that tell the computer hardware what to do.

Proofreading carefully reading what has been typed in and comparing it with what is on the data source (order forms, application forms, invoices etc.) for any errors, or just reading what has been typed in to check that it makes sense and contains no errors.

Protocol a set of rules governing the format of the data and the signals to start, control and end the transfer of data across a network.

Proxy-server a server which can be hardware or software that takes requests from users for access to other servers and either forwards them onto the other servers or denies access to the servers.

Query a request for specific information from a database.

RAM (random access memory) type of main internal memory on a chip which is temporary/volatile because it loses its contents when the power is removed. It is used to hold the operating system and the software currently in use and the files being currently worked on. The contents of RAM are constantly changing.

Range check data validation technique which checks that the data input to a computer is within a certain range.

Read-only a user can only read the contents of the file. They cannot alter or delete the data.

Read/write a user can read the data held in the file and can alter the data.

Real-time a real-time system accepts data and processes it immediately. The results have a direct effect on the next set of available data.

Real-time processing type of processing where data received by the system is processed immediately without any delay. Used mainly for control systems, e.g. autopilot systems in aircraft.

Record the information about an item or person. A row in a table.

Relational database a database where the data is held in two or more tables with relationships (links) established between them. The software is used to set up and hold the data as well as to extract and manipulate the stored data.

Relative reference when a cell is used in a formula and the formula is copied to a new address, the cell address changes to take account of the formula's new position.

Report the output from a database in which the results are presented in a way that is controlled by the user.

Resolution the sharpness or clarity of an image.

RFID (radio frequency identification) reader reads data from a small chip/tag at a distance.

ROM (read-only memory) type of internal memory on a chip which is permanent/non-volatile and cannot have its contents changed by the user. It is used to hold the boot routines used to start up the computer when the power is switched on.

Router hardware device which is able to make the decision about the path that an individual packet of data should take so that it arrives in the shortest possible time. It is used to enable several computers to share the same connection to the internet.

RSI (repetitive strain injury) a painful muscular condition caused by repeatedly using certain muscles in the same way.

rtf (rich text format) file format that saves text with a limited amount of formatting. Rich text format files use the file extension '.rtf'.

Rules base one of four parts of an expert system and made up of a series of IF, AND, THEN statements to closely follow human-like reasoning.

Sans serif a set of typefaces or fonts that do not use the small lines at the end of characters which are called serifs.

Scanner input device that can be used to capture an image; useful for digitising old non-digital photographs, paper documents or pictures in books.

Screenshot copy of what is seen on a computer screen. Can be obtained by pressing the Prt Scrn button and then a copy of the screen will be placed in the clipboard. The copy of the screen can then be pasted.

Search engine program which searches for required information on the internet.

Secondary storage storage other than ROM or RAM and is non-volatile, which means it holds its contents when the power is removed. It is used to hold software/files that are not instantly needed by the computer. Also used for backup copies.

Secure Socket Layer (SSL) see SSL.

Sensors devices which measure physical quantities such as temperature, pressure, humidity, etc.

Serial/sequential access data is accessed from the storage media by starting at the beginning of the media until the required data is found. It is the type of access used with magnetic tape and it is a very slow form of access when looking for particular data on a tape.

Serif a small decorative line added to the basic form of a character (letter, number, punctuation mark, etc.).

Smartphone a mobile phone with an advanced operating system which combines the features of a mobile phone with other mobile devices such as web browser, media player, Wi-Fi, camera, GPS navigation, etc.

Smishing using text messaging to send fraudulent messages that try to steal your credit card, banking or other personal details.

SMS (short messaging service) service that provides texting.

Social networking site a website used to communicate with friends, family and to make new friends and contacts.

Software programs controlling the operation of a computer or for the processing of electronic data.

Software licence document (digital or paper) which sets out the terms by which the software can be used. It will refer to the number of computers on which it can be run simultaneously.

Solid state backing storage the smallest form of memory and is used as removable storage. Because there are no moving parts and no removable media to damage, this type of storage is very robust. The data stored on solid state backing storage is rewritable and does not need electricity to keep the data. Solid state backing storage includes memory sticks/pen drives and flash memory cards.

Sound card expansion card consisting of circuitry that allows a computer to send audio signals to audio devices such as speakers or headphones.

Spam unsolicited bulk email (i.e. email from people you do not know, sent to everyone in the hope that a small percentage

may purchase the goods or services on offer).

Spellchecker program usually found with a word-processor and most packages which make use of text which checks the spelling in a document and suggests correctly spelled words.

Spyware software that is put onto a computer without the owner's knowledge and consent with the purpose of monitoring the user's use of the internet. For example, it can monitor keystrokes so it can be used to record usernames and passwords. This information can then be used to commit fraud.

SSL (Secure Socket Layer) standard used for security for transactions made using the internet. SSL allows an encrypted link to be set up between two computers connected using the internet and it protects the communication from being intercepted and allows your computer to identify the website it is communicating with.

Standalone computer if a computer is used on its own without any connection (wireless or wired) to a network (including the internet), then it is a standalone computer.

Storage media the collective name for the different types of storage materials such as DVD, magnetic hard disk, solid state memory card, etc.

Style sheet a document which sets out fonts and font sizes for headings and subheadings, etc., in a document. Changes to a heading need only be made in the style sheet and all the changes to headings in the document will be made automatically.

Swipe card plastic card containing data stored in a magnetic stripe on the card.

Switch a device that is able to inspect packets of data so that they are forwarded appropriately to the correct computer. Because a switch sends a packet of data only to the computer it is intended for, it reduces the amount of data on the network, thus speeding up the network.

Systems software programs that control the computer hardware directly by giving the step-by-step instructions that tell the computer hardware what to do.

Tablet a portable hand-held computer device that is primarily controlled via a touch screen.

Tags special markers used in HTML to tell the computer what to do with the text.
A tag is needed at the start and end of the block of text to which the tag applies.

Tape magnetic media used to store data.

Templates electronic files which hold standardised document layouts.

Terabyte a unit of file or memory size that is 1024 gigabytes.

TFT (thin film transistor) a thin screen used in laptops/notebooks or in desktops where desk space is limited.

Thesaurus software which suggests words with similar meanings to the word highlighted in a document.

Touch screen a special type of screen that is sensitive to touch. A selection is made from a menu on the screen by touching part of it.

Trackerball an input device which is rather like an upside down mouse and is ideal for children or disabled people who find it hard to move a mouse.

Transaction a piece of business, e.g. an order, purchase, return, delivery, transfer of money, etc.

Transcription error error made when typing data in using a document as the source of the data.

Transposition error error made

when characters are swapped around so they are in the wrong order.

txt text files just contain text without any formatting. Text files use the file extension '.txt'.

Update the process of changing information in a file that has become out of date.

URL (Uniform Resource Locator) another way of saying a web address.

USB (Universal Serial Bus) a socket which is used to connect devices to the computer such as webcams, flash drives, portable hard disks, etc.

User a person who uses a computer.

User interface one of four parts of an expert system that uses an interactive screen (which can be a touch screen) to present questions and information to the operator and also receive answers from the operator.

User log a record of the successful and failed logins and also the resources used by those users who have access to network resources.

Username or User-ID a name or number that is used to identify a certain user of the network or system.

Utility software part of the systems software that performs a specific task such as create a new folder, copy files, etc.

Validation checks these are checks that a developer of a solution sets/creates, using the software, in order to restrict the data that a user can enter so as to reduce errors.

Verification checking that the data being entered into the ICT system perfectly matches the source of the data.

Video cards circuits that generate signals that enable a video output device to display text and graphics.

Video-conferencing ICT system that allows virtual face-to-face meetings to be conducted without the participants being in the same room or even the same geographical area.

Virus a program that copies itself automatically and can cause damage to data or cause the computer to run slowly.

Voice recognition the ability of a computer to 'understand' spoken words by comparing them with stored data.

WAN (wide area network) a network where the terminals/computers are remote from each other and telecommunications are used to communicate between them.

Web logs (blogs) websites that are created by an individual with information about events in their life, videos, photographs, etc.

Web cam a digital video camera that is used to capture moving images and is connected to the internet so the video can be seen by others remotely. They are often included as part of the screen in computers or bought separately and connected to a USB port.

Web-conferencing service allowing conferencing events to be shared with users who are in remote locations using internet technologies. Usually there will be one sender and many recipients.

Web page a document that can be accessed using browser software.

Website a collection of interconnected web pages relating to a topic or organisation.

Wi-Fi a trademark for the certification of products that meet certain standards for transmitting data over wireless networks.

WIMP (windows icons menus pointing devices) the graphical user interface (GUI) way of using a computer rather than typing in commands at the command line.

WLAN a local area network (LAN) where some or all of the links are wireless, making use instead of infrared or microwaves as a carrier for the data rather than wires or cables.

World wide web (www) the way of accessing the information on all the networked computers which make up the internet. www makes use of web pages and web browsers to store and access the information.

zip a popular archive format widely used when downloading files from websites using the internet. ZIP files are data containers since they can store one or several files in the compressed form. After you download a ZIP file, you will need to extract its contents in order to use them.